KT-570-281

Managing Depression with Mindfulness

FOR

DUMMIES

A Wiley Brand

Cardiff Libraries
www.cardiff.gov.uk/libraries

Llyfrgelloedd Caerdydd
www.caerdydd.gov.uk/llyfrgelloedd

by Robert Gebka

FOR

ACC. No: 05030873

Managing Depression with Mindfulness For Dummies®

Published by: **John Wiley & Sons, Ltd.,** The Atrium, Southern Gate, Chichester, `www.wiley.com`

This edition first published 2016

© 2016 John Wiley & Sons, Ltd., Chichester, West Sussex.

Registered office

John Wiley & Sons, Ltd The Atrium, Southern Gate, Chichester, West Sussex, PO19 8SQ, United Kingdom

For details of our global editorial offices, for customer services and for information about how to apply for permission to reuse the copyright material in this book, please see our website at `www.wiley.com`.

All rights reserved. No part of this publication may be reproduced, stored in a retrieval system, or transmitted, in any form or by any means, electronic, mechanical, photocopying, recording or otherwise, except as permitted by the UK Copyright, Designs and Patents Act 1988, without the prior permission of the publisher.

Wiley publishes in a variety of print and electronic formats and by print-on-demand. Some material included with standard print versions of this book may not be included in e-books or in print-on-demand. If this book refers to media such as a CD or DVD that is not included in the version you purchased, you may download this material at `http://booksupport.wiley.com`. For more information about Wiley products, visit `www.wiley.com`.

Designations used by companies to distinguish their products are often claimed as trademarks. All brand names and product names used in this book are trade names, service marks, trademarks or registered trademarks of their respective owners. The publisher is not associated with any product or vendor mentioned in this book.

LIMIT OF LIABILITY/DISCLAIMER OF WARRANTY: WHILE THE PUBLISHER AND AUTHOR HAVE USED THEIR BEST EFFORTS IN PREPARING THIS BOOK, THEY MAKE NO REPRESENTATIONS OR WARRANTIES WITH THE RESPECT TO THE ACCURACY OR COMPLETENESS OF THE CONTENTS OF THIS BOOK AND SPECIFICALLY DISCLAIM ANY IMPLIED WARRANTIES OF MERCHANTABILITY OR FITNESS FOR A PARTICULAR PURPOSE. IT IS SOLD ON THE UNDER-STANDING THAT THE PUBLISHER IS NOT ENGAGED IN RENDERING PROFESSIONAL SERVICES AND NEITHER THE PUBLISHER NOR THE AUTHOR SHALL BE LIABLE FOR DAMAGES ARISING HEREFROM. IF PROFESSIONAL ADVICE OR OTHER EXPERT ASSISTANCE IS REQUIRED, THE SERVICES OF A COMPETENT PROFESSIONAL SHOULD BE SOUGHT.

For general information on our other products and services, please contact our Customer Care Department within the U.S. at 877-762-2974, outside the U.S. at (001) 317-572-3993, or fax 317-572-4002. For technical support, please visit `www.wiley.com/techsupport`.

Library of Congress Control Number: 2015960747

ISBN 978-1-119-02955-7 (hardback/paperback) ISBN 978-1-119-02957-1 (ebk)

ISBN 978-1-119-02957-4 (ebk)

Printed and bound in Great Britain by TJ International Ltd, Padstow, Cornwall, UK

10 9 8 7 6 5 4 3 2 1

A Wiley Brand

Contents at a Glance

Table of Contents

Part II: A Journey into Healing with Mindfulness 33

Chapter 3: You Really Can Heal and Recover!........35

Introduction

This book is for you if you are interested in exploring how mindfulness can support you in your efforts to regain, as well as maintain, your sense of wellbeing and happiness.

I wrote the book drawing upon my clinical experience as someone who has professionally supported people with depression both as a mental health worker in a psychiatric hospital as well as in private practice. More importantly, though, I wrote this book drawing forth on my personal journey of having not only suffered from depression but also having healed through it now living a life of meaning and happiness.

When you are in the midst of the storm of depression, it is incredibly difficult to see the possibility of happiness. It is my intention in this book to share ideas and practical techniques that are not only scientifically proven to work but that will help you regain your ability to manage your condition more effectively. This in turn will hopefully help you reconnect with your own sense of happiness and wellbeing. Above all, I trust that this book will offer you a beacon of light no matter where in your journey of healing.

I share the following words of inspiration from a client of mine who joined our 8-Week Mindfulness Based Stress Reduction course. She now works with autistic children and uses the mindfulness skills she learned to help others.

I had suffered with depression on and off for years. Anxiety was a feeling I fought daily. I have taken antidepressants and tried different therapies but nothing really worked for me. I attended a mindfulness seminar with a friend and although felt very uncomfortable at first there was something immediately that excited me, and I experienced a connection never felt before. I attended several classes and joined the 8-Week Mindfulness Based Stress Reduction course. The tools and experience have totally changed my life, and now I love sharing this with others. Learning to notice your thoughts and acknowledging them rather than challenging or attaching is such a powerful tool.

When faced with uncomfortable feelings, being able to believe and trust in yourself that by breathing into them you can reduce their intensity is very reassuring. It's also comforting to know that by focusing your mind on your physical body you can calm yourself. Three years on and mindfulness is a massive part of my life, and I'm so grateful for it finding me.

I invite you to take this journey with me as we explore what mindfulness is and how you can begin to embody it in your life.

About This Book

This book is for you whether you are suffering from depression yourself, caring for someone who has the condition or are a health professional wanting to know more about how mindfulness can support your clients recover from low mood and chronic unhappiness.

Scientific studies now show that you can use mindfulness to change the way your brain works. Regular mindfulness practice makes you smarter and wiser and so better able to deal with what life throws at you. When you are depressed you can often feel like you have no control and no say in how and what you think and feel. With regular practice you can gain back the control and learn to live your life with more compassion and skill where your mind is your friend rather than your enemy.

Use this book in a way that works for you. You can read it chapter by chapter or dip into in and out of it as you like. It is important to remember that this book is simply an introduction to mindfulness and I hope that you will eventually find the inspiration to seek out a mindfulness teacher or join a mindfulness course to help you explore a daily mindfulness practice. Above all, don't put any pressure on yourself to remember any of the ideas covered in this book but rather do what comes naturally and easy for you.

Following are just some of the topics I explore in this book to help you understand what mindfulness is and how you can use it to support your own sense of wellbeing:

 ✔ The anatomy of depression as well as some of the common symptoms and types of depression

✔ How to begin to recover from depression mindfully and explore some of the barriers to recovery and how to work through them these

✔ The basic mechanics behind mindfulness as well as how the mind works from a mindfulness perspective

✔ Self-compassion and how to develop loving kindness towards yourself

✔ The blessing within depression and how you can find meaning amidst difficulty

✔ Nine mindful attitudes that will help you live a happy and meaningful life and prevent depression from coming back

Foolish Assumptions

I assume, or rather I trust, that you or someone you know or care for has some experience with depression. I also work on the understanding that you have reached out and are exploring ways to help yourself heal through depression mindfully. In other words, I trust that you feel ready to help yourself recover from depression and regain your sense of wellbeing. I understand that it is possible that you know nothing about mindfulness or that you might have some knowledge of the subject. It is also possible that you have already explored other approaches and want to deepen the way you work with your own mind and life using mindfulness.

I also assume that you are not currently clinically depressed, or that if you are, you have other psychological support in place to supplement your healing and recovery.

Note: If you are currently suffering from severe or clinical depression, contact your chosen health professional before trying any of the exercises in this book.

Icons Used in This Book

Like other *For Dummies* books, this one has icons in the margins to guide you through the information and help you zero in on what you want to know. The following paragraphs describe the icons and what they mean.

This information is useful and worth keeping in mind when working with your experience of low mood and depression.

The text next to this icon is particularly useful information offering quick and effective ideas to support your learning about mindfulness.

I include some examples to help demonstrate and clarify different ideas and models that I present in this book.

This is an opportunity for you to try a practical exercise which will help you develop a greater sense of awareness leading to wellbeing.

Beyond the Book

This book is bursting with content, but you can go online and find even more. Check out the book's online Cheat Sheet at www.dummies.com/cheatsheet/managingdepression withmindfulness. And you can find a handy bonus article related to managing depression with mindfulness at www.dummies.com/extras/managingdepressionwith mindfulness.

Where to Go from Here

Although you can certainly get loads of guidance by reading from Chapter 1 through to the end, I designed this book so that you can dip in and out as you like, reading bits that you find most useful at any given time. If you feel you need some quick and easy-to-implement tips on how to enhance your sense of wellbeing, go directly to Chapters 12 and 13. If you feel you need to gain some motivation to help support you directly on your journey to healing mindfully, Chapter 3 might be a good start. To help you locate relevant material easily elsewhere in the book, I use cross-references as well as a comprehensive index, so feel free to explore these tools too.

The biggest benefit of mindfulness comes when it becomes a daily way of life. It might also be useful to remember that you don't need to struggle alone learning it. It is best learned with the support of a teacher or coach. I hope that this book will support you to eventually reach out and connect with a person or mindfulness-based group for the purpose of learning, growing and healing.

Above all, see this book as an exploration with nothing to lose but everything to gain.

Part I

Understanding Depression and Befriending Your Life

getting started with

managing depression

For Dummies has great info on lots of different topics. Check out www.dummies.com to find out how you and learn more and do more with *For Dummies*.

In this part . . .

- ✔ Discover how to befriend the black dog of depression and learn to turn off negative thoughts.

- ✔ Explore the major types of depression, as well as some possible causes.

Chapter 1

Your Journey to Wellbeing

● ●

In This Chapter

▶ Getting to know your big black dog of depression

▶ Knowing that you're not alone in your depression

▶ Seeing the link between depression and anxiety

▶ Understanding that recovery from depression has ups and downs

▶ Finding inner peace through the practice of mindfulness

● ●

*I*f you are reading this book, then it is very likely that either you or someone you know is affected by depression. I know from personal experience having lived with the condition myself that it can be very tough and that often it's difficult to get out of bed, to say nothing about reading a whole book. In my own experience, I have been where there was no hope and no guiding light at the end of the tunnel with very dark thoughts about my future constantly on my mind barking like hungry dogs that haven't been fed for days. You might or might not relate to this. I am writing this book both as someone who has first-hand experience living with depression as well as someone who has counseled many people affected with this condition both in private practice as well as within an inpatient psychiatric hospital setting. More importantly, I am writing this book as someone who recovered from the condition.

Above all, I am writing this book as a happy person, a truly happy person. I am not bragging about my happiness, not at all, but I like talking about wellbeing and happiness as this is the other side of the deep and wide river, the other shore, so to speak. This is where you too want to get to, don't you? The other side of the river where there is more light, more hope, more freedom to live your life as you want and desire. Recovery from chronic unhappiness has many stages and it's an up-and-down process, but I know that it is possible. This book offers a practical guide which will empower you to navigate the often confusing landscape of your own mind and give you plenty of tools for working with it in a way that can help you enhance your sense of mental and emotional wellbeing and happiness. I hope you will enjoy this journey with me.

Befriending the Black Dog of Depression

Having depression is in many ways like having a black dog. No offence to black dogs as they are lovely animals. However, you can use this as a metaphor for how difficult life can be when you are depressed.

This black dog of depression isn't just any black dog. It's a big and scary dog (shown in Figure 1-1), and having this dog around is a pain.

© John Wiley & Sons, Inc.

Figure 1-1: Depression as a huge black dog.

This black dog of depression looks extremely sad. Whenever he shows up he can make you feel completely empty of any happiness. He makes you feel slow, tired and not wanting to do anything except sleep. He can make you feel old, useless and hopeless.

Everyone else seems to be enjoying life, but you are only limited to seeing the world through the black dog's dark sunglasses. Life looks dark and bleak. Things that you used to enjoy don't give you any pleasure anymore. This black dog of depression robs you of your concentration, and you seem to not only forget things but you don't remember what it feels like to be happy either.

Doing normal daily tasks seems impossible as you are dragging this heavy dog behind you. You know that you have this black dog always with you even though others might not see it. The thing is you are really afraid that others might find out. It is likely that you might feel a deep sense of shame, and so you try to hide it from others, afraid that others will judge you if they ever found out.

This can make you feel like you are false, like you are a fraud in some way. Having the black dog probably ruins your appetite, and you either don't feel like eating at all or you overeat to try and shut him up. It's possible that he wakes you up at night and barks all the negative thoughts viciously into your fragile mind, making you stay up at night.

Above all, the harder you try get rid of the black dog of depression the bigger he becomes. You try to run away, but he follows you. You try to self-medicate, but that doesn't always help either.

Below are the some of the ways the big black dog can make you feel. In other words, these are some of the symptoms of depression:

- ✔ Moving or speaking more slowly than usual
- ✔ Change in appetite or weight (usually decreased, but sometimes increased)
- ✔ Lack of energy and extreme tiredness
- ✔ Lack of interest in sex
- ✔ Feeling hopeless and helpless
- ✔ Continuous low mood or sadness
- ✔ Feeling guilt-ridden
- ✔ Difficulties in concentrating and making decisions
- ✔ Using excessive alcohol or drugs to help you cope

✔ Isolating yourself and staying at home for days on end

✔ Taking part in fewer social activities

✔ Losing a sense of connection with the people around you

Go to Chapter 2 for the complete list of symptoms and possible causes of depression.

Things can get better, and you can recover from depression. The fact that you are reading this book means that your journey to healing has already began. Mindfulness can help you not only make sense of this black dog of depression, but also give you ways to get your life back by helping you to manage your thoughts and emotions more effectively.

You Are Not Alone – One in Four Have Depression

When you're depressed you may feel like you are the only one who has the problem and that everyone else is happy and normal. This kind of feeling, although very normal, can cause you to feel extremely isolated and causes you to suffer in silence. The truth is that many people who look happy are in fact also depressed and chronically unhappy. There are more of us than you might think.

Looking at it this way can sometimes help you feel a little bit better about your situation, knowing that you are not alone in with your problem.

The World Health Organization predicts that more people will be affected by depression than any other health problem by the year 2030. It is no surprise then that about one in four people suffers from some kind of mental health difficulty such as depression.

You might find it interesting that many famous people have suffered from depression as well. This just shows that depression is more common than you might think. Below are a few names of famous people who suffered from depression at one point in their lives. You might recognise some of them:

✔ Stephen John Fry, English actor, presenter, and activist

✔ Charles Dickens, British writer

- Eric Clapton, English musician

- Eminem, American rapper

- Bob Dylan, American singer-songwriter, poet and artist

- Ruby Wax, American comedienne

- Robbie Williams, British pop singer

- Sir Winston Churchill, British Prime Minister

- J.K. Rowling, British writer

You might think that you are less of a person or in some way bad because you are depressed. This is not true! Depression is an 'equal opportunity condition' and affects all classes of people. Anyone can develop depression. Practising mindfulness regularly can not only prevent depression, but it can also help to treat it. So there is hope you can recover and, with time, regain your sense of wellbeing and happiness.

The biggest challenge with depression is to reach out for support. Research shows that people who ask for help recover much faster than those who don't. It can be hard to reach out, but you can do so safely by speaking to your doctor, a trusted friend or a counselor.

Anxiety and Depression – Always on the Same Bus

According to the UK Mental Health Foundation, around half of those people who experience depression will also experience anxiety. This means that to some extent depression and anxiety go together. They are like two best friends always on the same bus.

Anxiety and depression are not the same, but they often occur together. People with depression often experience anxiety, and people with anxiety often become depressed.

For many people having the two conditions can be a temporary situation. For example, you can experience

- A temporary bout of depression after a severely stressful or anxiety-provoking event

- Temporary anxiety following an episode of depression

However, some people suffer with both of these difficulties at the same time for most of the time.

The link between anxiety and depression is so strong that most antidepressants are used to treat both anxiety and depression at the same time. This is partly because research suggests that the same neurotransmitters may also play a role in causing both anxiety and depression.

Practicing mindfulness helps with both calming the mind as well as helping you to balance your mood. Research shows that mindfulness practices can significantly reduce anxiety and depression. Not only that but Mindfulness Based Cognitive Therapy (MBCT) is significantly more effective than antidepressants alone in preventing relapse from depression.

Healing Is Possible – But It Takes Time

With the right support recovery from depression is possible. It is useful to remember that any healing through depression takes time and is often met with an up-and-down process of lows, highs, stable periods, lows again, then more stable times leading to another improvement and feeling better (see Figure 1-2).

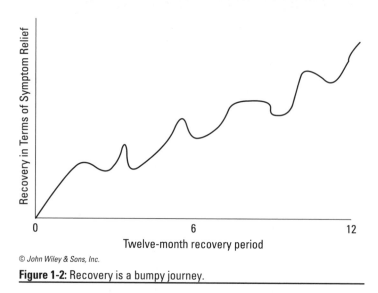

© John Wiley & Sons, Inc.

Figure 1-2: Recovery is a bumpy journey.

As much as we may want it to, wellbeing often does not happen overnight. It is normal to want to speed things up or to worry that you will never feel better. The thing to remember is that with time and the right support your symptoms will improve, and you will feel better.

Very often we do not notice any improvement, mainly because we can't see how far up the line of recovery we actually travelled. It's human nature not to notice positive changes. Also it is possible that each time we feel low on our journey to recovery we mistake it for failure rather than an opportunity to reflect and learn from the experience.

As hard as it can be sometimes, try to remind yourself that Rome wasn't built in one day. It has taken a long time for your condition to materialise, and it might take some time for you to learn mindfulness skills that will help you manage your mood more effectively and feel better. Seeing things this way can help encourage the feeling of hope.

Chapter 3 explores some of the difficulties that you are likely to encounter when recovering from depression and offers ideas how you can begin to enhance your sense of wellbeing.

Finding Inner Peace through Mindfulness

In many ways you can say that mindfulness is a state of mind as well as a state of being. In other words, mindfulness is how you truly relate to your very own life and existence. Mindfulness meditation originates within the Buddhist reflective tradition and is translated as awareness. Awareness of your inner and outer life. In other words, it's the awareness of what happens.

- ✔ Internally, in terms of your thoughts, feelings, sensations, and memories

- ✔ Externally, such as the things you see, hear, smell, taste, touch, or anything that you come into contact with in the outside environment.

It is useful to know right from the start that any explanation of mindfulness only points you to the door of actually experiencing it. You cannot think yourself into being mindful. You can only experience it by going through a process of doing an actual mindfulness exercise.

Using mindfulness to turn off from negative thoughts

Another way of looking at mindfulness is using the example of when you are lost in worry or when you are lost in some painful emotion. You probably have experienced this at one point or another in your life.

You wake up in the morning and just know that it's not going to be a good day, right? Do you know this feeling? I bet you do! Your mind is racing with fearful thoughts, your body feels tight and sore with painful sensations and you feel anxious, sad and somewhat irritable.

What happens then is that you may end up trying to think yourself out of the situation and so you go round in circles hoping to resolve the problem. However, the worry or struggle simply persists and you feel worse for it.

This kind of compulsive thinking is called *negative rumination* or *brooding* or *negative self-talk*. Research into depression shows that negative rumination is both a symptom of depression as well as the very thing that contributes to making it worse.

So what this means is that you have to find a way to reduce this obsessive negative self-talk. By doing so you can then enhance your chances of not only reducing depression but also enhancing your sense of wellbeing, happiness and inner peace.

Following are just a few examples of negative self-talk or rumination thoughts (we all have our personal ones):

- ✔ I am useless and hopeless.
- ✔ I will never get better.
- ✔ I am stupid and will never find happiness.
- ✔ The man in the bank looked at me funny because he knows that I am worthless.

So how does mindfulness come into play? How can you begin to find inner peace and freedom from worry, stress and depression through the practice of mindfulness?

Note here that I said 'through the practice' not through the thinking about mindfulness.

On a most basic level mindfulness helps you to step away from this negative rumination and shift your focus and attention to the five physical senses.

In order to find inner peace, you have to be willing to drop the thinking and the struggle and experiment with this technique. In other words, mindfulness helps you to return your attention to the body where you can experience more stability and balance.

Most of us in the modern society are stuck and lost in our heads, constantly analyzing and planning or going through the past dwelling on things. People with depression dwell more on the past rather than frantically planning for the future. Any future planning is done in a negative defeatist way, thinking and feeling that your future might be hopeless and pointless.

Mindfulness can help you bring more balance to this obsessive quality and help you live more in the present, where the real power and happiness can be found.

Why is this so? Why is it that you can begin to find greater inner peace by being more aware of your body and five physical senses? One reason is that the body is more solid and easier to anchor your attention on. There is a science behind this which is explained in Chapter 4.

Trying out a mindfulness exercise

To demonstrate this idea of returning your attention to the body, try the following mindful eating exercise and simply notice what you experience:

1. **Get yourself an orange or a mandarin and sit quietly on a chair.**

2. **Take some time to settle down and take a few deep breaths and allow for things to calm down.**

3. **Take the fruit in front of you and look at it.**

   Examine its shape, the colours, its smell and so on. Simply allow your mind to focus on the fruit in front of you.

4. ***Slowly* begin to peel the fruit.**

   Piece by piece, notice what you sense in your fingers. You might at this time also be aware of a smell which might also evoke certain feelings, most probably pleasant, but whatever they are simple notice and register them without preference.

   Continue with the peeling of the fruit very slowly.

5. **Once you have peeled it completely, take a piece and put it near your mouth.**

   Notice the effect of that. Do you sense your stomach beginning to prepare for digestion? Do you feel saliva coming down in your mouth? What else can you sense and feel?

6. **Slowly start eating the fruit.**

   Really slow down the eating and take time to actually taste the fruit itself. What you do feel? What is the taste like? Is it sweet or sour? Do you like or dislike the taste? Do you want to rush through it, or can you remind yourself to do it slowly and mindfully?

7. **Now simply allow your eyes to close for just a moment and stay with all the sensations – the smell, the taste, the sensation of touch and whatever else you can experience.**

   Notice your mood and thoughts as well.

Now take a moment to reflect on what you have experienced. How was this for you? Did you feel different after the exercise? If so, what was different? Where was your mind during the exercise? Was it more in the five physical senses, or was it more in thought?

Mindfulness is a practice, and just like anything new that you learn it takes time. With regular practice you can begin to live less in your head and more in your body. By being more in your body you can have the freedom to navigate through life in a more skillful and effective way.

Chapter 2

Understanding the Anatomy of Depression

In This Chapter

▶ Understanding what depression means to you

▶ Getting to know your symptoms

▶ Getting the right support for your situation

*A*s someone who has suffered with and healed through depression using mindfulness, I know how useful it is to have at least some understanding of the condition.

Understanding your condition a little bit better greatly supports you in your efforts to get well and stay well. I believe that the more informed we are about what is happening to us the more empowered we can be to do something about it, rather than suffer in isolation and silence.

Having supported people with depression using mindfulness-based interventions, both in private practice and within a psychiatric hospital setting, I know that the best way to heal through this condition is to apply the attitude of collaboration. This means that you and I work together to help you get better. In other words we both use our efforts to support you in developing a greater capacity for self-management, healing and recovery.

This chapter provides helpful information on depression and invites you to explore what depression means to you. I will look at the different types of depression and possible causes of the condition as well as providing a quick and practical symptom checklist to help you make sense of your own unique situation. I trust that you will find this chapter of benefit on your journey to greater emotional wellbeing.

Understanding Depression – A Balanced View

So what is depression? Well, the truth is that there isn't really a universally accepted definition of depression, and no one knows for certain what exactly causes it either. Depression is more defined according to signs and symptoms and how severe they are.

So if you are experiencing certain symptoms, one of them being persistent low mood, then you might be said to be experiencing depression.

It depends on whom you ask about the condition, their training and what model they use to define and inform them about depression.

If you go to your medical doctor, he or she might tell you that depression is a brain condition or illness which happens because your brain is not making certain chemicals called neurotransmitters. If you ask the same question of a psychologist, he or she might give you a completely different answer, most probably that depression is connected to how you think and process and express your emotions.

Some new research suggests that the most helpful way of looking at depression is through a more balanced and integrated model which takes into account the whole person and not just focusing on one aspect of the human expression.

We can say that depression has causes and symptoms which are usually experienced in combination on the following levels, namely:

- **Biological** or physically such as our bodies

- **Psychological** or in our minds such as our thoughts and feelings

✔ **Environment** such as our living conditions

✔ **Behavioural** or our lifestyle and the way we act and behave

✔ **Social**, our in our human relationships and connection to others

In other words, depression can be caused by different factors and there is a usually a connecting link between them, as shown in Figure 2-1.

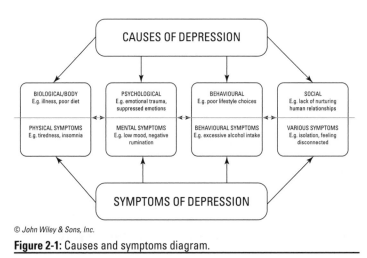

© John Wiley & Sons, Inc.

Figure 2-1: Causes and symptoms diagram.

Mindfulness helps you to be more in tune with your life and focuses on helping you to manage your thoughts, emotions and behaviour more effectively. It deals more with psychological and behavioural aspects of depression such as helping you to feel more grounded and so reducing the excessive unhelpful thinking called *negative rumination*, in this way empowering you to make better choices. You can find more about this in Chapter 5.

In other words, this book will help you to learn techniques that will help you reduce negative rumination and take achievable steps towards managing and healing through your condition more effectively.

Mindfulness helps you to be more aware of what other areas of your life might need to be examined. These might include:

- ✔ **Your environment, such as your living conditions.** For example, living in a noisy environment with lots of pollution can contribute to or worsen your condition.

- ✔ **What you eat, such as your daily diet.** For example, eating processed food excessively can lead to a depletion of nutrients necessary for proper brain function, which can contribute to depression and low mood.

- ✔ **The absence of good, supportive, nurturing human relationships.** For example, not having friends or family who can support you in life can also contribute to loneliness, low mood and even depression.

Recent research suggests that this kind of recovery based approach and integrative method of healing is more successful in helping you get and stay well as opposed to only using antidepressant medication.

How Bad Is It? Severity, Intensity and Frequency

Depression is not just having the occasional sadness that you can snap out of. There is a big difference between the occasional low mood or sadness and the persistent feeling of hopelessness and inability to function. You can say that sadness is a natural response to change and certain situations in life, such as the loss of a loved one, for example.

Depression, on the other hand, has symptoms which can be more persistent and potentially debilitating and is classified according to:

- ✔ How severe your symptoms are or to what degree they interfere with your life

- ✔ Their intensity or how strong they are

- ✔ Their frequency or how often they occur in your life

The condition of depression is generally divided into mild, moderate and severe. You might relate to the below examples.

You can cope but are not happy: Mild depression

In mild depression you might be able to get on with your daily life and most of the demands placed on it, but you are just not feeling right and you are struggling. Your energy might be low, accompanied by anxiety, you might be feeling low in mood for no apparent reason and you are just not enjoying life as much as you would like. You are, however, able to deal with this in some way using your own coping strategies.

Mindfulness can help you discover ways to work with your thoughts, mood and behaviour in a way that enhances your ability to self-manage your condition.

Struggling to function: Moderate depression

If your depression is moderate then you might be feeling like your ability to cope with daily tasks is strongly affected. Doing the most simple things such as going to work is very difficult. Your sleep might be badly affected and you might feel like your mind is just going in circles thinking negative thoughts which makes all things worse. Moderate depression is similar to the mild form but much worse.

Mindfulness can still help you in this situation but it is helpful if you seek professional help such a counsellor or a trained mindfulness professional.

I can't function: Severe depression

In severe or clinical depression – also called *major depression* – you might feel like you just cannot cope at all and go on. You have no energy to eat or do the most basic things. Working might be impossible and you might even have persistent thoughts or impulses about ending your life. This form of depression might feel like a total collapse of your mind and body and requires medical attention.

Mindfulness should only be used under clinical supervision in this kind of depression as it can potentially make your condition worse. You have much greater chances of recovery if you see your chosen health professional for support.

What Type of Depression Do I Have?

There are many forms and types of depression, each with commonly shared symptoms as well as symptoms that are unique to the type of depression.

 Try to remember that most of the time you don't know that you are depressed and that it is okay if you feel confused as to what is actually going on. By clarifying your situation you can begin to make greater sense of your condition.

Below are some of the main types of depression and some possible causes behind them. You might relate at least to some of the examples.

Too much stress – Depression due to chronic stress

Evidence is increasing that *chronic stress* (stress which goes on for a long time) can lead to depression. As humans, we can adapt and meet the challenges placed upon us, but there comes a point where we can no longer cope with excessive stress, causing a kind of collapse which can lead to low mood and possible depression.

Food for the brain – Low mood due to nutritional deficiencies

Excessive consumption of foods with low nutritional value, such as sugar and junk food, can deplete your body of important nutrients that are necessary for proper brain function. This can potentially lead to or contribute to depression.

The search for meaning – Existential distress

Some people who are deeply sensitive might feel that life is not making sense anymore. This is where questions about the reality of life, meaning and purpose might become apparent and there is a kind of spiritual quality to this experience. People who are experiencing this might feel confused about their place in life and feel unfulfilled in some way. This kind of spiritual distress can be often misinterpreted and misdiagnosed as depression.

My body hurts – Depression due to illness

Physical illness which seriously affects your ability to enjoy life and causes you physical pain can cause you low mood and potential depression. So if you have been diagnosed with an illness then it might be worth finding extra support to help you manage the emotional effects of the illness.

Too much change – Low mood due to extreme life changing events

Situations such as the loss of a job or death of a loved one can potentially cause anxiety and depression. This form of low mood or distress is usually a healthy reaction to a difficult life situation and usually passes once the situation changes in some way or you find a way of coping with it. At times the process of grieving becomes stuck as people find it hard to go through the different stages of grieving; it is here that depression can set it.

Give me light – Seasonal Affective Disorder (SAD)

This condition is cause by the lack of sunlight and usually affects people who work night shifts and in countries that have long winters or where there is absence of natural sunlight. One theory is that lack of sunlight makes the brain produce too much melatonin, a naturally occurring chemical in the brain that causes sleepiness and helps people fall asleep at night. Another theory is that lack of sunlight causes low production of serotonin, another chemical made by the brain that affects mood and level of wellbeing.

Before and after having a baby – Pre- and post-natal depression

Most pregnancies go smoothly and there can be excitement as well as some anxiety about giving birth. This is a normal response shared by most women. At times, however, some women experience severe anxiety and low mood either prior or after giving birth. The actual cause of this is complex but might have something to do with hormonal changes, previous depression and contributed by potential problems within the family and perceived lack of support.

Living with trauma – Depression due to abuse

Childhood mental, physical and or sexual abuse can create a lot of pain not only for the child during the abuse but also later in adult life when the incident becomes buried and in some ways forgotten. Such an experience can cause feelings of shame, guilt, anger and rage which often becomes suppressed, potentially leading to depression.

It's in my genes – Genetic predisposition

In some rare cases there can be a predisposition to depression, especially if it runs in one's family. You must understand, however, that just because there is a genetic predisposition does not mean that you will be affected by the condition. Also there is no way of testing for this kind of predisposition so thinking that it is in your genes does not always empower healing and recovery. You can still protect your mental wellbeing by taking good care of your mind and body.

The severe mood swings – Bipolar disorder

This is a more serious form of depression where people have days feeling extremely elated or happy and energetic and other days feeling utter hopeless, extremely low in mood and depressed. The cause of this condition is yet unknown but some research suggests that it might have something to do with a brain chemical imbalance with other factors such as extreme stress and early childhood trauma.

Medication – Mood changes due to side effects of medication

You might be experiencing changes in mood and possible depression due to some of the medication you are taking. Some pain medication in particular can have this side effect so it might be worth to check with your medical practitioner if you are currently taking medication for another health condition.

I just cannot go on – Major or clinical depression

This is a very severe and debilitating type of depression which at times can come on without any known reason. Sometimes mild to moderate depression when untreated can turn into severe or clinical depression. Again the causes can vary and usually it is a combination of factors. In extreme and rare cases, depression can also turn into psychosis, a form of severe mental illness.

In order for you to be diagnosed with clinical depression you must be experiencing certain debilitating symptoms which are present for at least two weeks.

Making Sense of My Symptoms – Self-CheckList

As mentioned earlier, your symptoms might be expressing themselves on different levels such as in your body, your mind, your behaviour and within your social relationships or your interaction with others.

Depression is experienced differently for different people but there are some common symptoms to all. Please note that the symptoms described below can also be part of life's normal lows. When these symptoms are a few in number and have been there for some time and are negatively affecting your life, it is very likely that you might be experiencing depression. If in doubt always contact your chosen health professional for a diagnosis and further support.

This section offers a breakdown of most of the general symptoms of depression. It might be useful to check whether you can relate to any of them and identify which ones apply to your unique situation.

Your body – Physical symptoms

When we are experiencing depression our body often also feels unwell. We can have all sorts of unexplained pains and problems that can be connected to our low mood. This is not a complete list but you might be able to identify with at least some of them.

❑ Moving or speaking more slowly than usual

❑ Change in appetite or weight (usually decreased, but sometimes increased)

❑ Constipation

❑ Unexplained aches and pains

❑ Lack of energy or lack of interest in sex

❑ Changes to your menstrual cycle

❑ Disturbed sleep (for example, finding it hard to fall asleep at night or waking up very early in the morning)

Our mind – Psychological and emotional symptoms

One of the most striking symptoms of depression is the way we feel and think. Our mood can be extremely low and it can be very difficult to have the motivation to do anything. Below are just some of the psychological symptoms of depression.

- ❑ Feeling hopeless and helpless
- ❑ Continuous low mood or sadness
- ❑ Having low self-esteem
- ❑ Feeling tearful
- ❑ Feeling anxious or worried all the time
- ❑ No motivation or interest in things
- ❑ Lack of enjoyment in life
- ❑ Feeling guilt-ridden
- ❑ Feeling irritable
- ❑ Difficulties in concentrating and making decisions
- ❑ Having suicidal thoughts or thoughts of harming yourself

Our actions – Behavioural symptoms

When we feel unwell, our way of life changes, we don't do the things we used to enjoy anymore and often we develop other behaviours such as self-medicating and drinking alcohol to help us get by. You might relate to some of the symptoms below.

- ❑ Using excessive alcohol or drugs to help you cope
- ❑ Losing interest in your hobbies
- ❑ Avoiding challenges
- ❑ Not doing well at work and staying off sick
- ❑ Isolating yourself and staying at home for days on end
- ❑ Having difficulties in your home and family life

Our relationships – Social symptoms

Depression can also adversely affect the way we interact with and relate to other people. People with this condition usually become very isolated and withdrawn, which often leads to a worsening of the condition.

❑ Taking part in fewer social activities

❑ Avoiding contact with friends and family

❑ Loosing a sense of connection with the people around you.

❑ Choosing friends that are not good for you

❑ Entering into destructive relationships

❑ Isolating yourself from others and the world

Exploring Your Own Experience

As you are exploring what is going on for you, you might benefit from some mindful self-reflection.

Depression has some commonly shared symptoms, but you are a unique individual and your situation might be expressing itself differently.

By exploring the following questions you might begin to understand how things are for you personally and so begin to gain more clarity, which will help you along your journey to healing and recovery.

❑ Do you feel that you relate to the ideas described in this chapter?

❑ Can you relate to the different types of depression?

❑ Do any of the symptoms described in this chapter apply to your situation?

A Word of Caution – Extra Support

The biggest challenge in terms of recovering from depression is to reach out for help. We might feel in some way vulnerable and afraid of criticism or that we should not be feeling down, that we should be stronger.

At times you might perhaps feel afraid of what your friends and family might say if you told them. You might even feel like there must be something so wrong with you that no one would want to help you.

These are all normal symptoms of depression and if you are feeling like this then this is perfectly okay.

It is important, however, that if you are feeling suicidal or struggle to cope that you tell someone, either your medical practitioner or by going straight into your nearest A&E (Accident & Emergency) hospital department.

Alternatively you may wish to get in touch with The Samarians, an organisation which provides confidential support.

Telephone: 08457 90 90 90 or visit its website: www. samaritans.org.

One Thing You Can Do to Continue Healing

I wish to congratulate you as the very fact that you are reading this book means that you are beginning to support yourself more skillfully. I hope that you will continue reading the book and find ways to support your own journey to recovery.

Mindfulness can help you live well with your condition. Since the mid 1970s just under 30,000 medical patients suffering from serious life-limiting conditions, including depression, have gone through the 8-Week Mindfulness Based Stress Reduction (MBSR) programme. Mindfulness Based Cognitive

Therapy (MBCT) is also endorsed by the NHS (UK's government free National Health Service) and approved by NICE, or the National Institute of Health and Clinical Excellence for the prevention of relapse of depression.

One thing I would like to invite you to do is to simply take a deep breath and begin to acknowledge the possibility that you are already healing. How does this possibility feel? Is there acceptance or resistance to this or something else? Simply notice what it is and let it be as it is now.

Part II

A Journey into Healing with Mindfulness

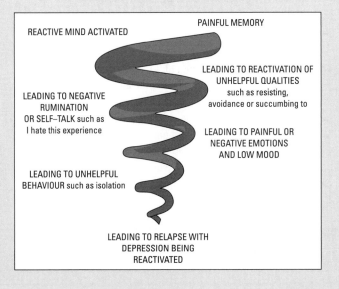

REACTIVE MIND ACTIVATED

PAINFUL MEMORY

LEADING TO REACTIVATION OF
UNHELPFUL QUALITIES
such as resisting,
avoidance or succumbing to

LEADING TO NEGATIVE
RUMINATION
OR SELF–TALK such as
I hate this experience

LEADING TO PAINFUL OR
NEGATIVE EMOTIONS
AND LOW MOOD

LEADING TO UNHELPFUL
BEHAVIOUR such as isolation

LEADING TO RELAPSE WITH
DEPRESSION BEING
REACTIVATED

web extras

Check out this book's online Cheat Sheet at www. dummies.com/cheatsheet/managing depressionwithmindfulness. Get helpful tidbits on topics such as scientific backing for the use of mindfulness in treating depression, statistics to prove you aren't alone in your journey of healing from depression and more.

In this part . . .

✔ Find out how to cultivate the attitude that recovery is possible.

✔ Understand what mindfulness is and how to use it to avoid living life on autopilot.

✔ Get introduced to the notion of the compassionate observer and gain tips on how you can effectively work with negative thoughts.

✔ Examine some of the qualities of the mind that make you more stuck on your head and gain empowerment through techniques that can help you bring your mind more into the present moment.

✔ Become familiar with self-compassion and how it can be cultivated in your own life.

Chapter 3

You Really Can Heal and Recover!

. . . .

In This Chapter

▶ What healing and recovery from depression means to you

▶ Understanding and working with barriers to healing and recovery

▶ Shifting from 'suffering from depression' to 'living well with depression'

. . . .

*W*hen we are depressed our motivation is usually very low and we don't always feel like doing anything about it. The most important tasks, such as paying bills, can be hard enough for us to do, so finding the necessary motivation to get better might not come so easy. We might even feel like we are not in a position to recover, not because we don't want to, but because we feel we are not able to. Having said that, there might be times when we feel our mood is at a reasonable level. This is when we could consider exploring the subject of mindful healing, not by forcefully challenging ourselves to make ourselves feel better, but through the process of exploration and discovery.

In this chapter, I invite you to simply travel with me through some of these helpful ideas. Together we will journey through some concepts that you might just be interested in. If you are, you might even be inspired to consider trying them out for yourself. Above all, please don't feel any pressure to do any of the exercises if you don't feel like it, but simply follow your own capacity and interest and do what comes most naturally to you. This chapter offers some inspiration and possible hope, and provides some ideas for how you can begin to recover from depression mindfully.

Healing and Recovering from Depression

Healing and recovery means finding creative and skilful ways of working with and managing your condition. It does *not* mean trying to get rid of it, but rather beginning to live well with it so that we have more freedom to enjoy life despite our difficulty.

It might be useful to decide yourself what healing and recovery means to you, as it means different things to different people. To some it might mean being able to socialise more, while to others it might be getting out of the house and going for a walk once a week.

Rather than accepting other people's goals and aspirations for your recovery, I invite you to explore and decide this for yourself.

My own depression started in my early teens and I remember when I was in my final year of high school when I suffered a major depressive episode. My whole world came to a standstill. Since that time it has been a major battle and the journey through it was met with ups and downs. At one point I admitted myself to a hospital following a type of suicide attempt. I felt absolutely hopelessness and ashamed, feeling like nothing would ever get any better, like I had no future left to look forward to. I was in complete darkness and despair.

Looking back at my situation I feel that there wasn't one single thing that has helped me turn things around, but having said that, there was one idea that has helped me greatly in my recovery. This was the idea that I can begin to develop a sense of self-compassion towards all those aspects of myself that I was ashamed of and was so desperately hiding from.

I realised somewhere along the lines that my shame and self-hatred contributed greatly to my suffering and once I understood that, I knew that this was the most important thing to work on; in other words, I needed to explore what this idea of self-compassion was all about.

Approaching ourselves in a personal and unique way

Depression has some general characteristics, symptoms that pretty much anyone suffering from this condition experiences. For example, you might feel extremely isolated and find it hard to have any energy for doing your daily tasks, or you might sleep a lot during the day. Depression, however, is also a deeply unique experience with feelings and problems that only you the person can understand. This is because each of us is a unique individual with our own personality, needs and history.

Your journey through depression and the process of recovery is also in many ways a uniquely personal experience. So it might be helpful to avoid comparing yourself with others and simply do what works best for you at any given moment.

Exploring our needs and clarifying our goals

To begin to explore what mindful healing and recovery could mean for you, it might be helpful to simply take a moment and perhaps explore your current needs. In other words, what is the most important thing for you right *now*? Once you have a little bit of awareness of this, you might then be in a much better position to formulate a clear and achievable goal for yourself. This will then act as your support on your journey to healing and recovery.

Some of the things that can be of importance to you are:

- ✔ Improving your sleep pattern
- ✔ Getting out more
- ✔ Understanding how to relieve difficult emotions
- ✔ Caring more about what you eat
- ✔ Looking after your body better
- ✔ Beginning to function better
- ✔ Enhancing your mood levels

After gaining a clearer idea of your immediate needs, you can then ask yourself what small, achievable and sustainable steps you could begin to consider towards achieving your goals. What could one of these steps be for you?

Scientific Evidence for Using Mindfulness for Depression

Mindfulness is now an evidence-based technique used widely by the NHS (the UK's free public National Health Service). It is also endorsed by NICE, or the National Institute for Health and Care Excellence, as an approved therapy for the prevention of relapse of depression.

Numerous clinical studies demonstrate the effectiveness of using mindfulness for people suffering from anxiety and depression.

Below is an outline of just a few of such scientific studies:

- ✔ Mindfulness practices have been shown to significantly reduce anxiety and depression, both in the general population and in a variety of health conditions, including cancer, chronic pain, major depression, bipolar and anxiety disorders (Chiesa & Serretti, 2010; Evans et al., 2008).

- ✔ Mindfulness Based Cognitive Therapy (MBCT) is significantly more effective than antidepressants alone in preventing relapse from depression (patients with a minimum of three episodes) (Teasdale et al., 2000; Ma & Teasdale, 2004).

- ✔ Several studies have found MBCT to help during the course of a depressive episode. MBCT reduced depressive symptoms from severe to mild in one trial (with no change in a control group) (Barnhofer et al., 2009; Kenny et al., 2007).

- ✔ Studies looking at long-term changes in the brains of experienced meditators and those undergoing mindfulness meditation training. An 8-week Mindfulness Based Stress Reduction (MBSR) course results in actual physical changes in the brains of meditation novices. These manifest as increases in grey matter (brain cell bodies) concentrations in brain regions involved in executive reasoning (frontal cortex), learning and memory (hippocampus as above), emotion regulation, self-referential processing and perspective (Holzel et al., 2008; Holzel et al., 2010).

Neuroplasticiy – We Can Change Our Brain

When we are anxious, stressed or depressed, a part of the brain called the *amygdala* (shown in Figure 3-1) is overactive. This is the more primitive part of the brain that is associated with strong emotions such as fear and anger as well as the fight, freeze or flight stress reaction.

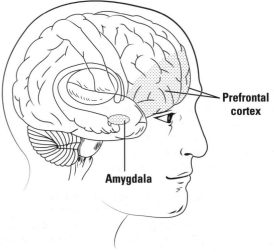

© John Wiley & Sons, Inc.

Figure 3-1: Parts of the brain affected by stress and depression.

Functional magnetic resonance imaging or *functional MRI* (fMRI) scans show that this part of the brain is overactive in people who suffer from stress as well as chronic depression.

The other function of the amygdala is that it overrides any logical thinking ability of the brain. Our ability to think rationally is partly governed by the *prefrontal cortex* located just behind the forehead (also shown in Figure 3-1). The reason why we find it extremely hard to make rational decisions when we are depressed is because the amygdala part of the brain overrides the prefrontal cortex, making us entrapped in our negative thoughts and emotions.

This is why doctors always recommend that people do not make life-changing decisions when feeling down and depressed. We are simply not able to think rationally and potentially end up making bad decisions.

Until recently scientists have believed that there was not much we can do using the power of our own minds to bring about positive physiological changes in the brain.

Recent studies in neuroscience, however, discovered that this old belief is not true and that with systematic training such as mindfulness practice we can in fact change our brain function.

This capacity of the brain to adapt, grow, change and develop is called *neuroplasticity*. 'So how does this translate to mindfulness and depression?' you may ask.

When we practise mindfulness we not only decrease the overactive amygdala part of the brain, but we also activate and increase the part of the brain associated with reasoning, decision making and self-control, called the prefrontal cortex. This again has been demonstrated by medical science via the fMRI scans which I mentioned earlier.

What is amazing is that this part of the brain increases in density in those people who have taken part in the 8-Week MBSR or Mindfulness Based Stress Reduction course. What is even more surprising is that this change in density occurs already at week 5 of the 8-week course.

What this means is that this part of the brain grows in size, density and functional connectivity.

So what does this all prove, you may ask? Well, it proves that you can, with proper mind training such as mindfulness, change your brain physiology. When the brain changes on a physiological level this automatically shows itself on a psychological and emotional level with a decrease in depression symptoms and increase in one's mood and sense of wellbeing.

Knowing this alone can be of immense benefit when we feel that we have no control over our thoughts, feelings and emotions and are doomed to a life of misery. Medical science has now demonstrated, whether we believe it or now, that we can change our brain and therefore with time, patience and consistent practice we can also ease our depression and learn to live well with it experiencing more ease, freedom and happiness.

Regaining Perspective

Often when we experience intense suffering we might feel like no one understands our pain, as if our pain is the deepest and most important of all pains. We might also feel like we no longer know where the depression begins and where it ends. So if we do feel like that it's completely okay and we can find reassurance that this too is part of the condition of having depression.

This is my pain, how dare you challenge it!

As I stated earlier, depression is a very personal experience, but having said this it is also shared by many individuals. According to the World Health Organisation (WHO), around 350 million people of all ages suffer from depression. The WHO also predicts that more people will be affected by depression than any other health problem by the year 2030. This means that you are not alone; I must be honest and say that when I suffered from depression this was the last thing I wanted to hear, for someone to tell me that I am not the only one suffering from depression. This was because as far as I remember it felt so deeply personal to me and in a way I didn't want anyone to challenge the way I related to it. You might or might not also experience a similar feeling.

There is a hindrance, though, to holding on so tight and seeing your suffering as so deeply unique and your own. The downside of this kind of attitude is that you block off any potential for personal growth, as you are not in a position to consider any possible change in your point if view.

The benefit of seeing our condition from both sides

If you can begin to simply consider that depression and suffering is not only personal to you but is also shared by many other people then you can begin to see your difficulty from a different angle. This might then help you accept your situation more easily and stop fighting it as you will take comfort in the reassurance that you are not alone in your pain.

Keep reminding yourself of the fact that depression is a common mental health condition and see if you can somehow reach out for more support. Consider speaking to a trusted friend or your chosen healthcare provider.

What Is Mindful Healing?

Mindful healing, in a nutshell, means having the willingness to get to know our condition, the very situation of depression and begin to consider working with it with more understanding, skill and compassion, rather than fighting it, resisting it or denying it, and so intensifying the pain and suffering.

Giving ourselves permission to heal

It is very natural to fight, resist or try to run away from painful situations. This is human nature. After all, no one likes pain or discomfort; we usually want happiness. However, the paradox is that the more we react to our situation of depression, either by fighting it or running away from it, or just giving into it, the more difficult things eventually become. Having said this, I wish to offer reassurance that it is absolutely normal and okay to find ourselves feeling like this. This is part of the experience of experiencing depression.

Often when we suffer from persistant low mood and chronic unhappiness we do so in silence and can feel ashamed, feeling like we should be able to just get over it and just be happy. It is okay to feel like this, but in the long end this is more of an obstacle to healing and recovery and only intensifies the difficulty.

Trying again, but in a different way

You might have tried many things to 'get over' your depression from medication to recreational drugs to drinking alcohol, to simply forcing yourself to be happy. Mindful healing, however, requires that you consider looking a little deeper and tune into and connect with your inner resources and wisdom in a way that feels safe, stable, supported and sustainable.

In some ways you have to first come to terms with the fact that you are experiencing depression, so there is a kind of 'risking' and vulnerability that is required. Although at first this is not easy, eventually this kind of making peace with the fact that you are depressed and feel like crap is immensely liberating: it will potentially enable you to shift into more tolerance and even acceptance of your difficult situation.

Turning our attention towards our condition

In order to begin healing mindfully, and this can feel counterintuitive and rather uncomfortable at first, we need to turn our focus towards the situation, not by obsessing and trying to fix it, but rather by beginning to find the courage and skill to befriend that which we have for so long rejected. In other words, we need to give ourselves permission to heal, permission to embark on this journey of self-discovery. Now, this idea of befriending might be quite challenging for some of us – and you know what, that is absolutely okay. Rome was not built in one day and all that I am inviting you to consider is taking small, manageable steps as guided and suggested in this book.

So what does giving permission to heal from depression mean to you?

> ✔ Does it mean continuing reading this book?
>
> ✔ Does it mean talking to someone you trust about your situation?
>
> ✔ Does it mean seeing a health practitioner of your choice?

✔ Or maybe it just means that you will go outside today and take a deep breath of fresh air as opposed to staying inside the house in isolation.

It might be something completely different for you so I invite you, if you care to, to simply take a few moments and reflect on what giving permission to heal might mean to you.

Relieving conflicting and difficult emotions

When our mood is very low we might be experiencing deeply conflicting feelings that might be extremely difficult to bear and even feel irreconcilable. We might feel like we will never be able to be happy again because we are not in position to make those feelings go away.

Considering the unthinkable – Connecting with our Wise Mind

Often when we experience depression the light of hope can be very dim if present at all. Things might be so tough that we have no place we can go for relief or for refuge from our pain and distress. At times like this when our situation is seemingly hopeless it can be immensely helpful to explore the idea of what we call 'Wise Mind' in mindfulness.

This idea originally comes from the Buddhist reflective tradition but has recently been adopted and rediscovered within psychiatry by Dr Marsha Linehan, who founded a therapy called DBT or Dialectical Behavioural Therapy. This particular therapy is being used for people with various mental health conditions, including depression. She herself was deeply afflicted by mental health illness. Following her recovery and training she used her own experience of mental illness to develop DBT. She is an example of a person who has transformed her suffering and now benefits many people in similar circumstances.

This idea of Wise Mind is based on the understanding that at the very core of our mind, there is already present calm and stillness, and with that a naturally present capacity to tolerate, befriend and even accept any difficulty with skill, understanding and compassion.

The quality of the Wise Mind is that of a capacity to be with two or more conflicting emotions, such as love and anger or fear and feeling safe. In other words, we don't have to try and get rid of our inner broken parts in order to feel whole in some way. We work on our capacity to allow it to stay and by allowing it to stay we can begin to learn to stop fighting our feelings and allow emotions to be just as they are, which then paradoxically gives them the opportunity change and potentially dissolve.

To know that we don't have to get rid of our inner broken parts can be so immensely liberating and can in many ways bring back the hope that we can actually learn to be happy again.

Consider the following exercise.

1. **Write on a piece of paper a short paragraph describing your problem.**

   You are writing to someone who is wise and has compassion, someone who would give you some reassurance and who understands your difficulty.

2. **Share your situation with that person and ask that individual to hold your problem for you.**

   This someone can be anyone from your past who has showed you some understanding or compassion or it can be an imaginary person or even someone like a counsellor or a spiritual teacher.

By doing this you are considering the unthinkable, namely that someone like this exists but also and more importantly you are considering that this kind of quality also exists within you.

Whether you believe or feel it at this moment in time is not important; what is important is that you perhaps take a moment to reflect on this.

Allowing for things to be as they are – The mindful paradox

This sounds crazy, right? How can things get any better if you let them just be as they are? Is this some kind of a crazy wisdom or what?

Well, in mindfulness there is this paradox – namely, that if you can allow yourself to get to know the situation just as it is with more accepting awareness, you then are in the best position to understand how to begin to work with it and manage it better.

In a similar way as when you put your hand in the aquarium, the kind you keep gold fish in and begin to stir the water, you will shortly notice that the sand turns into a water cloud which then makes it difficult for you to see and make sense of anything that might be inside. But if you stop stirring and be patient for the sand and water to settle down you will start seeing more clearly all that is inside: the rocks, the fish and the plants – and in this way you will have a better understanding of what is going on.

Noticing our relationship to our condition

So when it comes to working with and managing depression we can simply begin to learn to notice where we are at with things or to put in a different language to get to know what our relationship is to the depression.

There are three main ways in which we can relate to depression: we can either deny that we are experiencing it, we can fight and resist it by trying to get rid of it or we can succumb and give into it. These, by the way, are all normal and healthy reactions and I want to reassure you that it is okay to feel like this.

Imagine that your depression is a person. What would he look like? How tall would he be? What would he be wearing? What would his face look like and once you get an image then simply sense how you feel towards this image.

Do you like or dislike it, do you have understanding or perhaps anger and disappointment that it is there in the first place?

Simply notice what your reaction to your depression is; don't try to change it or make it better, but simply allow it to be as it is.

The more you can notice where you are at and how you feel in relationship to your difficulty, the less reactive you will become and the more capacity you will have to feel a sense of tolerance, acceptance and compassion for yourself.

Learning to live well with our condition

How can this idea of living well help us in managing our depression? As stated before we often fight our condition and in the process end up simply making it worse. So here we will benefit by adjust our attitude and with that our expectations of ourselves.

You might have to consider that your condition will never completely go away. This might be hard to hear and in itself potentially make you feel worse, but not necessarily.

What I am suggesting here is that you consider to explore ways that can help you stop fighting your present situation and support you to switch to a different attitude – namely to one of learning to live well with it. In other words, rather than wasting your efforts and energy to try and get rid of it you can adjust yourself and begin to take more creative steps to learn how to manage it more effectively.

This approach is very successful when working with people with chronic conditions; we know that many people will never completely be free from their afflictions but they can learn how to get to a point where they can manage it better and still enjoy a life of happiness despite their difficulty.

Exploring Some Barriers to Healing

Whenever we begin to consider learning something new we will most always encounter some resistance to change. This might come in many forms and is very normal and part of the process of recovery. The best attitude towards these inner barriers is to simply acknowledge them and let them be and leave them alone and remind ourselves why we are doing this journey in the first place. We don't have to try to get rid of the resistance but rather get to know it a bit more and simply bring our attention back to the process of learning mindfulness, developing a kind of curious attitude towards the experience of encountering resistance.

I cover a few of the common barriers in the following sections.

I don't really believe that I can heal

It's okay if you don't believe you can heal! You might have struggled with things for a long time, perhaps you have tried again and again and feel that you have failed because the depression is still here. So what happens at the end is a kind of giving up and resignation to the idea of ever feeling any better. Feel reassured that this is okay and part of having the condition.

You don't need to believe that you can heal, but what you need to be able to do is simply try risking again, this time not by trying to get rid of it but by learning skills and attitude that will help you manage things a little better. Seeing things this way can be of immense reassurance and will help lessen the struggle.

Who will I be without 'my depression'?

'We often have a hard time letting go of our suffering out of fear of the unknown, as we seem to prefer suffering that is familiar'.

You might feel that the above quote is harsh and in some ways lacks sensitivity to your situation, but there is a lot of truth in that. When we experience any chronic conditions there comes a point where our whole life gets affected by it and we form a personal identity and not only does the depression become ours but in some way we become the depression itself. Again this is normal and part of having this condition and it doesn't mean that there is something wrong with things being like that.

One of the challenges is to begin asking the question, who would I be if I was well? What would I be doing? How would your life be then? Doing this from time to time can help you develop hope, but don't worry if this does not come easy so the invitation is to, if you care to, to simply try it a few times and see where it takes you.

It's too much work and I am afraid to face my demons

Looking at our own life can at times be a daunting experience especially when we are not used to doing it. There can be a fear of becoming overwhelmed and not being able to cope with all the layers of emotion and sensation associated with befriending the situation of depression. So this type of fear is quite natural, but we can rest assured that mindful healing is more about doing whatever feels comfortable and safe.

Mindful healing is not about psychoanalysing ourselves or getting lost in difficult emotions, but rather using our naturally cultivated, non-judgmental awareness in a way that is helpful to our situation.

I tried to sort it out before and it didn't work

You might have tried many times to free yourself from the graps of chronic unhappiness. It's possible that some of your coping strategies have worked and some have not. It's part of the condition of being depressed to see everything as black or white, a kind of all-or-nothing quality of thinking. So it might be worth reexamining and noticing what has worked for you before. The mindful attitude toward healing is that you become aware of your goals but at the same time suspend them and simply focus on the process of learning mindfulness and then applying it to your situation. You need to allow things to unfold naturally for you. Depression is a complex condition and having too many rigid goals can be unhelpful.

So you can have goals but you mustn't feel bad when you don't reach them every time. Rather focus on learning from the situation and bring your focus to simply practising mindfulness.

Chapter 4

Understanding Mindfulness

In This Chapter

▶ Understanding the basics of mindfulness

▶ Using mindfulness to minimise negative self-talk

▶ Discovering the benefits of being more in your body

*M*y personal experience of living with depression has taught me that you can begin to find a way through it. I believe that with the right support you too can begin to discover ways that can be of help on your journey to emotional wellbeing.

Depression is complex, and as with any condition it can be challenging to begin to make sense of it, especially when you are in the midst of what can feel both like a storm and a mental prison. The prison walls can be very high and mighty, and any attempt to get out can meet fierce resistance. This was my own experience and is that of many people that I have coached over the years: you might perhaps relate to it.

We need to go slowly when looking inwards into our mental and emotional landscape. Being patient and giving ourselves time to get to know the mental and emotional knots that make up our depression can be of immense benefit. Practising mindfulness can support us in developing this very needed patience and self-compassion. It's as simple as taking a deep breath more often, wherever you are, and noticing what happens.

In this chapter, I offer an easy to understand definition of mindfulness and invite you to experiment with some practical tools that you can begin to apply in your own unique situation. Simply see this as an exploration and take from it what you need.

Developing the Willingness to Learn a New Way of Being

When we are feeling down and depressed our capacity to think in helpful and hopeful ways is dramatically reduced. We can feel like we are not in a position to make any changes in the way we perceive our inner and outer worlds. We can feel trapped and locked into our own emotional pain and sense of hopelessness. It is totally okay to feel this way and is part of having the condition. However, we still have our human capacity for choice and we can use this ability to begin to make sense of things and explore how we can potentially heal through our condition.

Our brains easily become set and stuck in certain ways of functioning, with specific brain networks being overactive and others underactive. However, *neuroplasticity* (the idea that our brains can adapt, grow and change) tells us that we have the capacity to positively affect our brain function as well as our psychological patterns.

The brain has a variety of networks or systems which have specific functions. You can compare this to electrical circuitry in a computer. People with depression have an overactive *Default Mode Network,* which can associated with a kind of constant negative thinking. This obsessive quality of being stuck in one's unhelpful thoughts and feelings is often referred to as *negative self-talk* or *rumination.*

Rumination is partly what is makes it so hard to make changes in the way we think, feel and behave. It's like we are stuck in a mental rut going over the same thing many times over. Mindfulness can help us to reduce this negative quality of mind by helping us bring our attention back to the five physical senses.

Having said that, the fact that you are reading this book probably means that you have become interested in how mindfulness can support your journey to healing through depression. This means that you have through your own effort activated a part of the brain called the *Task Positive Network,* which is associated with making choices.

This means that the willingness to discover new ways of thinking about your situation is already here. What might be helpful is to perhaps begin to recognise this.

Defining Mindfulness in a Practical Way

A few definitions exist of what of mindfulness is. However, we must from the point go understand that the theoretical definitions of mindfulness and the experience of mindfulness are two different things. However, understanding the basic theory behind mindfulness can be very helpful and is the first step towards actually experiencing it.

Mindfulness is an experience of being in a certain state of awareness and being. This can only be fully understood by doing the practice.

This way of looking at things can be very helpful as it will prevent us from having to try too hard at 'getting' what mindfulness is. We cannot 'get' mindfulness; we can, however, experience it.

Mindfulness has its origins within the reflective Buddhist tradition dating back to 2,500 years ago in India.

Figure 4-1 shows the Chinese calligraphy symbol for the western word mindfulness. The character is composed of two single sections: the top part is the word 'now' or 'present' and the second is the character for the word 'heart' or 'mind'. It's interesting that the Chinese word for the heart and mind is the same. In the Asian culture and language, mindfulness is seen more as the mind or heart that is resting in the present moment. The above character offers the true representation of it not just being a cognitive mind state or idea but more of a state of embodied experience of awareness.

© John Wiley & Sons, Inc.

Figure 4-1: The Chinese symbol for mindfulness.

Returning to our body – The five physical senses

Mindfulness is often defined as a kind of coming back to our five senses. I see this explanation of mindfulness as both metaphoric as well as literal and practical.

Most of the time we are lost in our heads, just thinking about the past, the future or just random stuff. We can spend a lifetime dwelling on the past in our heads. The interesting thing is that we are not even aware that we are this way. We function on a kind of automatic pilot going through life, unaware of what our minds are actually doing.

This is how it is for pretty much all of us and not only for those who are suffering with depression. People who are depressed, however, experience this quality of negative self-talk more often and much more intensely.

In one way mindfulness is about recognising that we function in this kind of way. We are in a way living in a dream often pre-occupied with our thoughts and feelings. The very recognition of this quality of mind can help us come back, but come back to where, you may ask?

 Have you ever had an experience where you were perhaps walking down the street joyfully unaware, just doing your thing? Maybe you were daydreaming or absorbed in thought or worried about something, and all of a sudden you heard a loud sound like a car hooting or someone calling your name? Quickly you became aware. All your attention shifted to that experience and you became fully aware of the sound. It is almost like you returned back to your senses of your own body.

If you can relate to this then this is what I mean by coming back to your five senses. In this example, you came back to the sense of sound but you could have easily smelled or seen or tasted or felt the breeze of the cool air that then brought you back to that particular sense.

So we have all to some degree or another experienced how we are lost in thought and feelings, simply unaware of our own body and the outside world, and we have also all experienced what it is like to come back to our senses.

The benefits of being more in your body

The benefit of being more in the five senses of the body is that we are as a result less stuck in our heads and so less preoccupied with our guilt, anxiety or our own troubles. Purposefully shifting our attention to the body will help us be less reactive and able to work with our situation more creatively and compassionately.

Other benefits include:

- ✔ Reduced negative rumination or unhelpful negative thinking
- ✔ Reduced emotional reactivity
- ✔ Increased sense of personal choice
- ✔ Increased clarity of thought

 ✔ Increased freedom from painful emotions

 ✔ Enhanced access to pleasant emotions

Stick with it! It can take a while before you can sense your attention in your body where the sensation and feeling is more neutral, so don't give up after one go. Practising mindfulness is like going to the gym: you need to do it regularly. Keep practising as often as you can.

The mindfulness chair

Another way of thinking about mindfulness is seeing it as a chair with four legs. The chair is stable and strong and all the four legs are equal in length and strength, so the chair can support your weight very well. In a similar way, when we cultivate the four elements of mindfulness we can experience a stable sense of awareness.

In the same way as our chair having four legs, mindfulness also has four elements to it and is often defined as the awareness that arises naturally when we:

 ✔ Pay attention in a particular way (First leg)

 ✔ Do so on purpose (Second leg)

 ✔ Do so in the present moment (Third leg)

 ✔ Do so with kindness and compassion (Fourth leg)

Let us explore these four elements or legs of our mindfulness chair in a little more details:

 ✔ **First leg: Paying attention in a particular way.** So we have this thing called attention. It's like a human given capacity: just in the same way we have the ability to walk so we have the ability to pay or direct our attention. That's the first thing we can say about attention. The way we direct, maintain and shift attention in mindfulness is through a relaxed non-striving, yet focused way. We are not trying hard to pay attention but rather doing it in an open, receptive kind of way.

 ✔ **Second leg: Paying attention on purpose.** We need to choose to pay attention and do it intentionally. This is because most of the time our mind functions on a default habitual automatic pilot, thinking either about the past or planning for the future. This means that being mindful doesn't come as a primary response and we need to purposefully cultivate it for our benefit.

✔ **Third leg: Paying attention in the present moment.** When practising mindfulness we are not psychoanalysing or trying to solve our past issues; neither are we strategising ideas for our future. Rather we are simply noticing what is happening, when it is happening. So let's say we experience a sad feeling rather than trying to understand where it came from. We simply notice it as a feeling. I explore more of this later in this chapter.

✔ **Fourth leg: Paying attention with kindness and compassion.** This means that we are not hard on ourselves when we encounter certain thoughts or feelings; in a way we can notice and perhaps even suspend the harsh self-judgements such as I am a failure because I am depressed. We can notice the self-judgements and be okay with and not judge ourselves for being judgemental.

Responding Rather than Reacting Habitually

'*Between stimulus and response, there is a space. In that space is our power to choose our response. In our response lies our growth and our freedom*'.

— Viktor E. Frankl

In life we can either respond wisely or react habitually to situation. It's worth exploring these two qualities of mind in a little more detail. In depression, being able to respond is more helpful than simply reacting to experiences habitually on automatic pilot.

Reacting on instinct or habit has its positive side, because it helps us to stay safe. For example, when we touch something hot we immediately pull our hands away from danger. This keeps us safe.

When it comes to managing and working with our thoughts, emotions and behaviour, whether it is related to depression or not, it is much more in our favour if we can begin to explore how we can respond with patience and self-compassion rather than just react habitually.

Following force of habit

We all have our own reactive tendencies and habitual ways of interacting to our inner (thoughts, feelings) and outer experience (life in general). The fact is that this is what makes us wonderfully human.

When we are depressed we often feel like we don't have a choice when it comes to our thoughts and feelings. It's almost as if we have collapsed in some way and don't challenge what we think anymore. This, however, is understandable and is part of having the condition.

Maybe you have had the experience where someone you knew was walking on the other side of the street, you waved at her and she didn't acknowledge you. Immediately you felt triggered somehow, with all sort of thoughts coming down at you in your mind such as: 'why didn't she greet me back, did I do something wrong? It must be me; you see, I'm not even worth saying hello to!' Following that, you probably felt quite down and low.

When we are anxious, stressed or depressed our tendency to react on automatic pilot is greater with the Default Mode Network part of the brain being more active than the Task Positive Network. In other words, gaining perspective on things can be more challenging when our mood is low.

Reactivity increases our unhelpful negative self-talk or rumination, which only makes us feel more depressed so we need to somehow begin to recognise when to react so that we can become more familiar with our own habitual patterns and practise switching to the Responding mind.

Responding and discerning: Exercising your options

Just like we have the capacity to react we also have the capacity and ability to respond more wisely to our thoughts and emotions, with greater discerning options and freedom of choice. It does take some practice and training, but if we consider how long we have been stuck on the reactive mode we can then begin to test this idea for ourselves with more patience and persistence.

Being able to respond means recognising that we have some choice in how we think and relate to our experience.

We can begin to reflect on the fact that we choose all the time: we choose what we eat, what we drink, what we watch on TV. This means that the capacity to choose is still here and we can start applying it to our condition of depression in order to minimise our unhelpful negative rumination and in this way enhance our emotional wellbeing.

With mindfulness we can train our minds to shift our attention from our reactions more towards the five physical senses. It is then when we have a gap, a little bit of freedom from our unhelpful thoughts and painful emotions. It is in that spacious gap where we can become aware of more helpful options and so choose to respond more wisely to our situation.

When we respond wisely, neurologically we reduce the over-active amygdala part of the brain which is partly involved in generating fear and anxiety. We are also activating the Task Positive Network part of the brain which partly involves the part of the brain called the prefrontal cortex, situated just behind our forehead. This part of the brain is responsible for what we call executive function and our ability to choose.

Functional magnetic resonance imaging (fMRI: a type of brain scan) shows that the prefrontal cortex part of the brain is severely underactive in people with depression. Regular mindfulness practice, however, can dramatically enhance prefrontal cortex activity.

Figure 4-2 shows a summary of the qualities and effects of both our responding and our reactive minds.

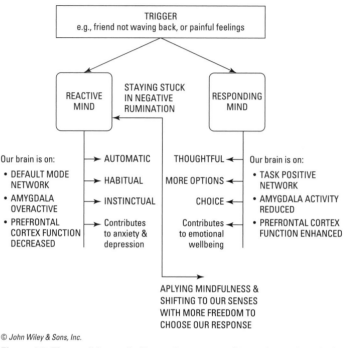

© John Wiley & Sons, Inc.

Figure 4-2: The qualities and effects of our responding and reactive minds.

Gaining perspective

Mindfulness helps us to gain more perspective on our thoughts, feelings and behaviour. Often when our mood is low we can feel overwhelmed and not know what we think or feel.

Shifting our attention from the messy state of mind to the direct experience within the body, where things are more neutral, gives us the opportunity to have some space and clarity of mind. In psychology, we call this *cognitive distancing* or *decentring*. It's a kind of freedom that potentially leads to emotional wellbeing.

This doesn't mean that all your problems will be solved in some magical way. Your unresolved issues will still be there, or whatever it is that is contributing to your depression, but you will be able to see more clearly with a sense of self-compassion and so gaining some freedom for the stormy emotional intensity that often accompanies the condition.

Putting Mindfulness into Practice – The ABC technique

Practising shifting our attention from our head and with that our tendency to engage in negative self-talk to our body and five physical senses will help us enhance our sense of well-being. This section shows how we can do it in practical terms.

Initially we might experience some resistance to doing this. This is basically the same reason why we feel resistance going to the gym. There might be many personal reasons for this resistance, but mainly it is due to it being a new experience and we are very used to doing the same old thing.

Trying out the following technique works best once we have practised the five-minute mindfulness exercises a few times so that we can get a feel for them. It might be work getting a mindfulness CD so that you can begin exploring the practice for yourself. Alternatively see Chapter 7 for an outline of short mindfulness practices.

✔ **A – Acknowledging:** We can begin to slowly step out of the habitual reacting or automatic pilot by simply acknowledging what is happening right in this moment, however uncomfortable. The simple recognition, validation and turning towards the discomfort takes the power out of it and in this way we can actually be aware that this is what we are doing. Developing the capacity to do this can, of course, take time and lots of patience.

So that is the first step. Whenever we feel stuck in a thought pattern or feeling or behaviour we can simply say, 'Hello. I see you. I might not like you, but hey, you are here'.

✔ **B – Breathe:** This is self-explanatory, and simply means that in the midst of being in whatever experience we simply take a deep, slow and comfortable breath. That's all.

When we get triggered and become anxious our breathing becomes shallow and fast so we are deliberately slowing it down so as to put a brake on.

The breath will also give us that space needed to have a little bit of distance, psychologically, from the automatic habit or rumination, and it is in that little bit of mental space that we take the next and last step, which is *connecting*.

✔ **C – Connect:** On a most fundamental level connect means connecting with your senses – sight, hearing, seeing, smell, taste, hearing. So rather than being caught up in mental worrying and negative rumination we simply shift our attention to the five senses and our body, such as the sensations in our feet or noticing what we see around us, such as buildings, the sky and so forth rather than continuing to be lost in our thoughts or our problems.

Figure 4-3 represents the ABC technique in an easy-to-remember way.

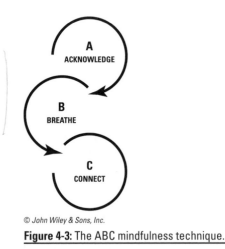

© *John Wiley & Sons, Inc.*

Figure 4-3: The ABC mindfulness technique.

Reacting is a normal human quality and we are not trying to stop ourselves from reacting. That would be putting too much pressure on ourselves. Rather we are beginning to be aware that we have reacted and then pick up the pieces, so to speak and see if we can switch to the responding quality of mind. In this way we minimise the automatic negative self-talk and enhance our capacity for feeling more grounded and in the body.

Get a coloured elastic band to remind you of your intention to practise mindfulness. You can also gently snap the band if you find yourself lost in rumination or need to come back to the awareness of your body. Be gentle though: don't snap it too hard.

Tips on how to be more in your body include:

- ✔ Ask yourself what you are doing right now.
- ✔ Ask where your body is right now and try to sense it.
- ✔ Ask what you can notice around you.
- ✔ Take a deep breath more often.
- ✔ Wiggle your toes and focus on the sensation in your feet or hands.
- ✔ Sway slightly from side to side as you are standing.

Mindfulness: Simple, But Not Easy

I know that I make doing the mindfulness practice in the previous section sound like it's a piece of cake. I also know from personal experience of living with depression that many days you might not even feel like getting out of bed.

Mindfulness is very simple yet not that easy to do, at first anyhow. This is true for pretty much anyone starting out. You can, however, simply give these techniques a try. Alternatively you might even see a mindfulness trainer to get some one-to-one coaching or join a mindfulness course.

Above all, be kind to yourself and see this more as an exploration, a journey into trying something new.

The Benefits of Being Patient and Tolerant

We can be very hard on ourselves when our mood is low. It's almost like our self-critical voice is shouting in our ear with a megaphone. When we start exploring mindfulness this self-critical part of us will most probably jump onto our train and try to tell us that we are not doing it right, this isn't working and I am stupid.

The radical thing to do here is to acknowledge and welcome this voice, give it a seat and say, 'Hello, I see you, I might not like you but you are here'. Once we give it permission to be as it is then with time and repeated practice its intensity will potentially reduce.

Chapter 5

Exploring Our Mental and Emotional Landscape

*D*epending on the type and severity of our depression we can either feel completely overwhelmed with negative thoughts and emotions, as if stuck in a storm, or we can in some way feel numb and cut off from our experience altogether, not being able to articulate or express what is going on inside our own mind. Is there a way that we can explore finding more balance in our emotional life, and if so then what can potentially help support us in this?

One thing that can help us make sense of our current experience is understanding the relationship between our thoughts, our feelings and how this relates to our mood levels and the way we behave. This is in many ways like having a map, a guide so to speak, which we can use to help ourselves navigate our internal experience. Mindfulness teaches us to be more of an observer to our thoughts, feelings and experience with a greater sense of loving kindness and compassion. Having a map can help us cultivate this compassionate observer self. By cultivating a sense of curiosity as opposed to getting lost in self-judgment, we can begin to unravel the numerous mental and emotional factors that contribute to the complex and personally unique experience of depression.

In this chapter, I invite you to explore how you can begin to work with your own experience in a way that fosters a greater sense of awareness and self-compassion.

The Idea of Responsibility: Being Able to Respond

It might come as a surprise to you to learn that there is a direct link between what and how we think and how we feel and behave. Taking the time to explore this link can give you the necessary skills to help you manage your condition more creatively and effectively.

For some people, beginning to reflect on this can be potentially uncomfortable because in some way it implies that you have some kind of responsibility for, or collaboration in, the way you feel and experience the world you live in.

I remember that in my early days of recovery, I was very defensive when someone implied that I was in some way responsible for being depressed, and I would take that implication very negatively, feeling like I was being judged. This was mainly because I felt completely powerless and didn't feel like I had any choice when it came to my thoughts and feelings. It was only later on that I was able to recognise that it was in fact *me* that was choosing, consciously or unconsciously, the mental attitudes and thoughts which contributed to my chronic unhappiness.

You need to understand the idea of responsibility not in terms of self-blame, by thinking that it is your fault that you are depressed, but rather with the understanding that your thoughts and the way you think contribute to your level of mood and mental wellbeing. In other words, leaning towards the idea if you can begin to think more balanced and realistic thoughts this will lead to more pleasant and hopeful feelings, which will help you experience a greater sense of wellbeing. Once you can begin to understand and accept this idea of being a collaborator with your experience you can then move forwards and learn how you can use this to your advantage.

Mindfulness Based Cognitive Therapy

You might have heard of a therapy called *Cognitive Behavioural Therapy* (CBT). CBT is based on an idea that our thoughts contribute directly to how we feel, which creates our mood and how we feel in turn contributes directly to how we act or behave. In other words, if we can think more realistically rather than negatively then this naturally leads to more pleasant and hopeful feelings and happy mood.

In the NHS, CBT is now the standard form of therapy used to treat most forms of mental health difficulties, including depression. MBCT or *Mindfulness Based Cognitive Therapy*, is a combination of the modern CBT technique and the ancient Buddhist form of mindfulness meditation dating back 2,500 years.

Clinical evidence shows that MBCT is significantly more effective than antidepressants alone in preventing relapse from depression and so supporting people to stay well for longer.

The main difference between MBCT and CBT is:

- CBT aims to challenge negative thinking patterns that contribute to what are called *negative feelings*.
- MBCT aims to help us ground ourselves in the body and observe our thoughts and feelings with more self-compassion.

Using CBT Language: The Basics

Understanding the connection between our thoughts, feelings and our mood can help us manage our condition more effectively. Often when we are depressed it can feel like one overwhelming experience, a kind of bigger-than-us feeling. By recognising that our thoughts affect our feelings, mood and behaviour, we can begin to gain some useful clarity on our experience so that it becomes less overpowering and more manageable.

Perhaps one of the greatest benefits of looking at our situation in this way is that it helps us to recognise that there is a process that takes place, a kind of mental chain reaction that leads to us feeling depressed. Relating to our condition this way can it more manageable. We can use the CBT model to help us understand this *connection* between *what* and *how* we think, our *relationship* to these thoughts and the *effect* that this has on our mood and behaviour. This section explains how using this model can help.

Understanding this chain reaction can help us to feel more in control and empower us take more collaborative action, rather than continuing to feel like a victim of our own circumstance.

The CBT model helps us understand this link in a very basic and generic way.

Firstly there has to be a *trigger*, or an event. In other words, something has to happen which sets off a chain reaction leading to certain *thoughts*. Depending on their quality, in other words, whether these thoughts are optimistic/realistic (positive) or pessimistic (negative), certain *feelings and mood* will follow. These feelings and mood in turn contribute to the way we *behave*.

Let us say you are very hungry one evening walking past a fish and chips shop and the smell (*trigger*) catches your attention. This will then set off *thoughts* in your mind, at first probably without you realising; in other words unconsciously, which might go like this, 'Wow, that smells good. Wouldn't it be great to just eat some of that!' This will in turn stimulate a certain *feeling* and *mood*. In other words, you might be really tempted to go and get the fish and chips. Finally this feeling and mood will then propel you into action, in this case buying the food and eating it, and hopefully feeling very satisfied. Especially if you like fish and chips. I know I do.

Figure 5-1 is a basic representation of the stages of how a trigger sets off a chain reaction leading to a certain behaviour. Each arrow represents the next stage in this process.

© John Wiley & Sons, Inc.

Figure 5-1: The cognitive behavioural model.

There is a complex interplay which takes place between our thoughts, feelings, moods, sensations and behaviour. Very often uncomfortable memories, sensations or feelings themselves can become triggers for certain ways of thinking about them. These in turn lead to us feeling low. So we need to remember that the trigger isn't always external such as an outside situation. In fact, in depression the trigger is often an internal one such as our own feelings, painful memories and painful sensations in the body. This can set off a further reaction which can worsen our mood.

Triggers can be both external such as someone saying something negative about our appearance – for example, leading to us feeling either angry or sad in some way, or the trigger can be an internal one such as a painful memory – for example, which then leads to negative thoughts and resultant low mood.

For example, you might wake up one morning being aware of a kind of anxiety or gripping fear in the base of your stomach. This can then set off a whole chain reaction of thoughts such as 'Oh no, I really don't want to feel this. This is my depression again. This is going to make me feel down, why today? Please go away!' which turn progresses into unpleasant and negative feelings and potential low mood.

In the preceding example, CBT works by examining these thoughts in more detail and finding alternative, more helpful and balanced thoughts which can replace the unwanted, negative ones. The more realistic and positive our thoughts can be, the greater the chances that our mood can improve.

Staying with this example, in mindfulness practice we acknowledge the effect that unhelpful negative thoughts have on our feelings and mood. We do not, however, unlike in CBT, aim to challenge our thoughts directly. The practice of mindfulness is based on the idea of the awareness and the observation of thoughts, feelings, memories and sensations. In other words, mindfulness places a greater focus on cultivating the compassionate observer self.

Rather than challenging your thoughts, feelings and sensations, during your mindfulness practice simply take time to explore what it would be like to simply observe them with greater tolerance and self-compassion.

Cultivating the Compassionate Observer

What mindfulness proposes is that it's not the thought, feeling, memory or sensation that causes us the pain or suffering but rather our reactive relationship to it. Mindfulness works not by aiming to change our thoughts and feelings directly, but rather by cultivating our capacity to observe them and relate to them in a more kind and compassionate way.

The more we begin to cultivate our capacity to simply observe our thoughts and feelings, the less identified we become with them and the more freedom we will gain from their negative effects which so often impact our sense of happiness and wellbeing.

It is very normal for people to struggle with their own thoughts and feelings, and it is understandable that we get stuck in negative mental experiences feeling that we are unable to break free. This is partly because most of the time we believe that our thoughts are facts. We hold on very tightly to our thoughts and feelings and make them very personal, which leads us to feel convinced that we are our thoughts. In other words, we struggle to see that thoughts and feelings are simply passing aspects within the mind, more like the clouds resting on the vast blue sky. It would be silly to say that the clouds are the sky. We know that the sky is larger and greater than any sum of clouds, or storms for that matter. Mindfulness suggests the same idea. It empowers us to cultivate a sense of spaciousness and awareness which can be compared to the vast blue sky.

Mindfulness proposes the idea that thoughts are not facts and even more than that mindfulness encourages the idea that you are not your thoughts. In other words, mindfulness helps you understand that you are not the clouds but rather vast blue sky.

Now this might be very challenging to relate to at first and even begin to consider especially when our mood is low. However, as we begin to explore mindfulness as a daily practice we begin to learn to step back from our thoughts and feelings and simply see these as passing aspects of our experience. It is this stepping back that gives us a sense of perspective and freedom from often difficult experiences. As we do this we start moving towards responding with more of a sense of choice and clarity rather than just reacting blindly.

 You are not your thoughts and feelings. You are so much more than that. With time and daily mindfulness practice you can begin to experience this greater sense of potential for yourself. It is possible and achievable, but it does take commitment to daily mindfulness practice with the support of a teacher.

Remember that mindfulness is about cultivating the compassionate observer whereas CBT is more about challenging the negative thoughts and finding positive alternatives. Both approaches work well with helping people recover from depression.

Qualities that contribute to depression: The reactive mind model

In Chapter 4, I explore the idea of the responding and reacting minds, and that being stuck in the reactive mind contributes to depression. I also explore the idea that neurologically, when we react we switch on the amygdala part of the brain, which is responsible for making us feel worse. Chapter 4 also introduces the idea that in depression the trigger is often an internal one: it can be a thought, a feeling, a memory or a sensation.

Another way of looking at the reactive mind is by recognising that it has certain qualities. These qualities increase our negative self-talk and so make us feel stuck in our experience. This ultimately leads us to feel worse.

In mindfulness we see that it's not the uncomfortable experience that causes us the suffering but rather the quality of our relationship to it.

There are three main unhelpful reactive ways of relating to our *experience*. By experience I mean our thoughts, feelings, memories and sensations.

We can:

- ✔ **Fight or resist:** In other words, we don't want the experience to be as it is, we struggle with it and we push it away in some way.

- ✔ **Succumb, or give into:** We in some way give in to the experience, almost as if being pulled into the pain.

- ✔ **Avoid:** We don't want to look at the problem. We put our heads in the sand and hope that it will go away.

The model in Figure 5-2 demonstrates the effects of the reactive mind on our experience. Each arrow pointing towards the circle (the trigger which can be thoughts, feelings, memories or sensations) symbolises an unhelpful reactive quality or relationship.

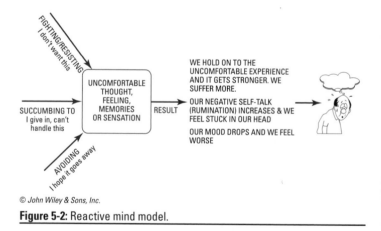

© John Wiley & Sons, Inc.

Figure 5-2: Reactive mind model.

What this means is that the more we resist, give into or avoid our uncomfortable experience, the stronger our negative self-talk and rumination becomes and the worse we end up feeling.

It is human nature to ruminate and most people struggle with their own thoughts and feelings. This is a natural human quality and it does not mean that just because you relate to your experience in that way that there is something wrong with you. This is simply how your mind works and mindfulness teaches you to simply acknowledge this mode of function, begin to recognise it and find a more creative and skilful way of working with it so that you may begin to respond with a greater sense of compassion and clarity rather than just react.

Qualities that contribute to wellbeing: The responding mind

Mindfulness teaches us to notice our experience by relating to it with a kind of non-judgemental curiosity. The very act of stepping back and noticing our thoughts, feelings and sensations is very therapeutic, and decreases our negative self-talk. In this way, it enhances our capacity to navigate through our emotional landscapes more creatively and effectively.

There are three qualities that belong to the responding mind; in other words, by consciously cultivating these attitudes we can begin to enhance our sense of happiness and wellbeing.

- ✔ **Staying in touch with our body:** This is the simple idea of being more in touch with our five physical senses. So in a way we are anchoring our attention in the body so that we can stay more grounded and less caught up in our heads.

- ✔ **Noticing with kind curiosity:** Here we turn our attention towards the experience, rather than pushing it away. We simply become interested in what is present in this moment, without analysing our thoughts, feelings or sensations, simply observing it with a soft, kind attention.

- ✔ **Allowing and befriending:** When we encounter an uncomfortable experience we can practise allowing it to be as it is: a bit like making friends with the difficult experience.

Figure 5-3 demonstrates the positive effects of relating to our experience with the qualities of the responding mind. Each arrow pointing towards the circle (the trigger which can be thoughts, feelings, memories or sensations) symbolises a helpful relationship to our often uncomfortable experience.

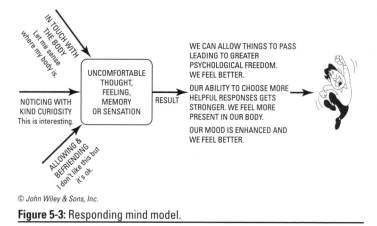

© John Wiley & Sons, Inc.

Figure 5-3: Responding mind model.

The more we keep in touch with our body and begin to notice our experience, allowing it to be as it is, the more capacity we have to live our life in the here and now, feeling better.

Mindfulness is a practice and what I am presenting here is just the theory behind it. It will most probably take time and support for you to be able to develop this capacity to relate to your experience with more awareness and self-compassion. It's the same as going to the gym: it takes time for us to see the benefits and we have to do it over and over again. So don't put any pressure yourself. Mindfulness is a process.

The mental filter of doom

When we are depressed we are very strongly and negatively influenced by certain mental filters or ways of thinking. These mental filters are like dark coloured glasses that filter and distort any light. These mental attitudes perpetuate the effects of the reactive mind and so keep us in a depressive cycle.

There are a number of them that CBT teaches us about and it might be worth referring to *Managing Depression with CBT For Dummies,* by Brian Thomson and Matt Broadway-Horner, for more information.

In my experience with depression the main mental filter that keeps us stuck in depression is the belief that

'Nothing will ever be okay again, my future is dark and bleak'.

When we have been thinking in this way for a long time it can feel impossible to make a change towards a happier state of mind.

The first step towards freedom from the effects of distorting mental filters is to notice them. Just acknowledge that the particular mental pattern is what is playing itself out and be kind to yourself in the process. The more aware you are of your thought patterns the less overpowered you will be by their negative effects.

Managing the depressive spiral using mindfulness

The more we practise mindfulness the greater our capacity becomes for noticing where and when we are reacting to our experience. It's not that we are aiming to be reaction-free. I have been practising mindfulness for nearly 15 years, and I still react often. At times I still feel down when I get triggered, especially when the trigger brings up certain painful emotions.

Part of my process of living mindfully is to allow myself to experience feeling low and create a safe space where I can begin to work with the low feeling using the skills that I have learned. Having a regular daily 5-minute mindfulness practice offers you this safe space, where you can cultivate a sense of awareness and self-compassion.

Try to remind yourself that healing through depression mindfully is not about forcefully preventing yourself from ever feeling low or depressed, but rather, using your mindfulness practice to begin to work with your experience more creatively and compassionately.

The idea is to simply notice when and how you react so that you can catch yourself and purposefully redirect your attention to the qualities of the responding mind, where you can rest more in the awareness of your body and of your five physical senses. In this way, with practice you can actually prevent yourself from going completely down and under and relapsing. Even if you do relapse that is totally okay and the best remedy for that is to simply allow it to happen with a sense of kindness where you simply do the best you can with what you have.

Figure 5-4 shows the usual way that our depression can become reactivated, leading to a relapse of depression with the spiral pointing downwards.

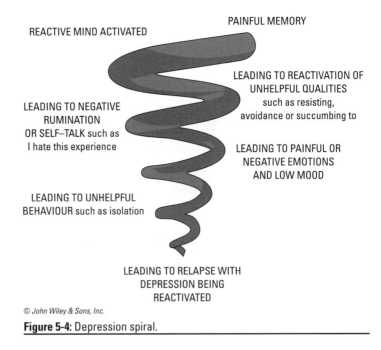

REACTIVE MIND ACTIVATED

PAINFUL MEMORY

LEADING TO REACTIVATION OF
UNHELPFUL QUALITIES
such as resisting,
avoidance or succumbing to

LEADING TO NEGATIVE
RUMINATION
OR SELF–TALK such as
I hate this experience

LEADING TO PAINFUL OR
NEGATIVE EMOTIONS
AND LOW MOOD

LEADING TO UNHELPFUL
BEHAVIOUR such as isolation

LEADING TO RELAPSE WITH
DEPRESSION BEING
REACTIVATED

© John Wiley & Sons, Inc.

Figure 5-4: Depression spiral.

What Is It All About?

Mindfulness is about practice. There are no quick-fix solutions, so we can right from the start let go of this idea that it's about a certain method that will fix all our problems. Anything that we do, whether it's CBT or going to the gym, takes time to develop, and unfortunately there are no shortcuts. It takes lots of patience and commitment, so don't feel like you have to remember all the things that we explore in this chapter.

If you remember one thing, then just remember to breathe more slowly and more deeply, more often, and with that simply bring your attention more towards your body.

Try the following exercise to help you concentrate on your breathing and on your body:

1. **Take a comfortable seat, sitting with your back straight and shoulders relaxed. Feel free to close your eyes if you like.**

2. **Begin by taking a few slow, deep breaths in your own way and your own time.**

   Do not worry about getting it right – simply breathe a little slower and a little more deeply.

3. **Now allow the breath to be as it wants to be.**

   Sometimes it will slow down even more, and sometimes it will speed up. Simply begin to notice how the breath is for you right now. Take a moment to notice it right now with a greater sense of acceptance and curiosity.

4. **Now bring some gentle movement into your feet.**

   You can wiggle or press down on your feet so that you can get a sense of them resting on the floor. Bring the movement to an end once you can get some sense of your feet and then simply rest your attention on the feet themselves. Start with one foot first and then the other. Simply become curious about what your feet feel like. Notice all the toes, the arch of the foot, the heel, the top of the foot, and so on. Do your feet feel cool or warm? Comfortable or uncomfortable? Tingly? Perhaps there is not much of a sensation at all. Just notice what the experience is in your feet.

If your mind takes you away and you get lost in worry or dwelling on the past or whatever the case might be, simply acknowledge that this has happened and bring your mind gently back to the awareness of your feet.

5. **Allow your attention to rest there for as long as it feels comfortable spending some time here.**

6. **When you feel ready to bring this meditation to an end, simply open your eyes.**

Chapter 6

Understanding the Rhythms and Qualities of the Mind

*M*aking sense of your thoughts and feelings can be very difficult, especially when you are feeling down and under. Often, we can be sucked into and get stuck in a whirlpool of strong feelings such as sadness, anger or fear, making it difficult to pull out and regain our perspective. The same can happen to us when we get lost in fast and racing thoughts, such as obsessive worry. Some people who are depressed can't feel much of anything, as if there was concrete cement poured into their brain numbing every feeling and emotion. Getting to know your own mind is a skill that can take time, and it is not an easy challenge to undertake. This is true even for those who do not have depression. It will, however, become easier once you have learned the basic mindfulness techniques and know how to apply them. With time, commitment and patience it is possible to begin to find a way through the vast territory of the undiscovered winds and storms of your very own mind and find ways of enhancing your mood and emotional wellbeing.

The beauty of mindfulness is that it gives you the very needed skills to support yourself in this process of inner exploration. In many ways it provides you with a map of how your mind works so that you can become more familiar with its complex dynamics. By becoming more familiar you can be more skilful in managing your own thoughts and emotions in a way that leads to greater ease, clarity and wellbeing. I offer this chapter as a compass and guide and hope that it will enhance your journey to finding inner peace.

Mindlessness – Being Lost on Autopilot

If you have ever flown in an airplane you will know that the pilot can choose to lay in a course by putting in details of a specific destination so that the plane flies on autopilot. This is very useful, as the pilot can then choose to focus on other aspects of flying or simply take a rest.

Well, guess what? Your mind is similar. As humans we also have the ability to function on autopilot. In a nutshell, *autopilot* means a habitual way of thinking and behaving that does not require conscious thought. It's all the stuff we do on habit and often unconsciously. Basically, anything that we learn that becomes an unconscious habitual response can be considered as an expression of the quality of autopilot, including riding a bicycle, eating, driving and so on.

You might have had the experience when you were driving your car somewhere. You arrived at your destination wondering how the heck you got there in the first place. It's like there was someone else driving while you were mentally doing the shopping list or still carrying out your job tasks that you didn't complete at work. Do you know this feeling? Well, this is the quality of autopilot, and we all do it.

What keeps the autopilot quality active and switched on is our unawareness of it. In other words, we are not aware that we are driving and daydreaming at the same time. The moment you become aware is the moment that you step out of autopilot and mindlessness into a mindful way of being.

Advantages and disadvantages of being on autopilot

Relating to the world on autopilot has its benefits, so I am not saying that there is something wrong with this quality of mind. It is natural and can have its positive aspects.

Functioning in this way can, at times, help us live more effectively in the modern world. It can help us to do two or more things at once – in other words, multitask. We can drive while making plans for the day. Our heartbeat happens on autopilot, so we don't have to think about it.

However, when it comes to dealing with our own internal mental experiences, such as thoughts, feelings and sensations, autopilot is not that useful, as it simply perpetuates our reactive quality rather than prompting a more skilful way of helping you to observe your thoughts feelings and emotions.

When on automatic pilot, we are more likely to have our 'buttons pressed'. Events around us and thoughts, feelings and sensations in the mind (of which we may be only dimly aware) can trigger habits of thinking that are often unhelpful and may lead to worsening our mood.

By becoming more aware of your thoughts, feelings and body sensations from moment to moment, you give yourself the possibility of greater freedom and choice: you do not have to go into the same old 'mental ruts' that may have caused problems in the past.

 Staying on autopilot keeps your negative reactions locked in. You can only bring about positive change if you can acknowledge what is out of place and identify what needs more compassionate attention. We need to realise the nature of this auto quality of the mind and bring in awareness if we are to initiate any meaningful and positive personal changes.

Two levels of autopilot

There are mainly two levels of autopilot. Put another way, there are two ways in which this quality of mind can express itself:

- ✔ Mental autopilot related to thinking
- ✔ Behavioural autopilot related to action

The mental habit is more like a computer program running constantly in the background. There are many such programmes running in our minds, most of them unconscious and without our awareness.

Following are the most common ones, which people with depression also have:

- ✔ Thinking about the past, usually regretting.

- ✔ Planning for the future in a pessimistic and negative way.

- ✔ Constantly evaluating, sorting and working out problems mentally.

- ✔ Having mental conversations with people who are not actually physically present. Everyone does this and this is different to hearing voices, which is what people do who are suffering from severe mental illness such as psychosis.

- ✔ This feeling that we need to be somewhere else than this moment where we are right now.

- ✔ Getting lost in non-specific random mental ideas, negative unhelpful thoughts and painful feelings

The second type of habit is connected to the way we behave or our actions. These unhelpful habits may affect our mood negatively.

These behavioural habits can be:

- ✔ Isolating ourselves when we feel low in mood

- ✔ Doing too many things at the same time

- ✔ Rushing around

- ✔ Taking too much to the alcohol bottle as a way of coping

- ✔ Taking mind-altering substances such as drugs, smoking to cope with discomfort

I invite you to begin to take time to identify your own mental and behavioural habits. What automatic tendencies do you get stuck in which perpetuate your chronic unhappiness?

Getting Back into the Captain's Chair

Let's come back to our example of driving. By contrast, 'mindful' driving is associated with being fully present in the moment, consciously aware of sights, sounds, thoughts and body sensations as they arise. In other words, you would notice things around you and know that you are driving rather than being stuck in a mental fantasy of daydreaming.

In many ways, the aim of mindfulness practice is to increase awareness so that we can respond to situations with choice rather than react automatically. We do that by practising being aware of where our attention is and by deliberately changing the focus of attention over and over again back to the five physical senses.

Understanding attention

Our capacity to have and to pay attention is an innate human ability. We are given this gift by the very default of being human. This means that we already have it and don't need to try very hard to create it. All we need to do is to begin to recognise this and work at taking small steps towards cultivating it.

You might have had the experience of when your attention was pulled by a pleasant smell, or maybe you saw something beautiful and suddenly all your attention was focused on that particular experience. Maybe you have been watching a favourite film on television, and all your attention was totally focused on the details of what was happening at hand. You might be able to relate to this. This means that in many ways you already know how to cultivate your attention.

 Mindfulness training is more like training the muscle of attention. The more you work at it, just like going to a gym, the better you get at pulling back your attention from painful experiences. It is this pulling back and redirecting of attention that helps you to get unstuck from being lost in your own emotional pain and discomfort.

Regaining your lost attention

Our attention is often pulled in or hijacked by the intensity of our own painful thoughts, feelings, memories and sensations. This is all the stuff we call bad or negative in some way.

You might have experienced being lost and stuck on certain uncomfortable feelings such as sadness or frustration. You know this gripping feeling of emotional pain which feels like a sensation of physical pain in the body, almost like an open emotional wound? You probably already know how difficult it can be for you to pull back to a place of balance and safety and how easy it is to feel overwhelmed by such an experience.

Our attention can get pulled in when our thoughts, feelings, sensations or memories are of a particularly painful quality. Our attention also gets pulled by pleasant thoughts, feelings and sensations, but this is not really a problem because it is an enjoyable experience.

It might be helpful to know that the more we are on autopilot, the more we are at risk of our attention being lost in our own uncomfortable thoughts and feelings. The opposite is also true. In other words, the more aware we are and the more in touch we are with our physical body and the five senses, the less caught up we will be with our own pain and inner discomfort. It is the getting caught up in our own stuff that then leads to overthinking, dwelling and negative rumination or negative self-talk, which then in turn contributes to your low mood and chronic unhappiness.

The mechanics of attention

Even though as humans we are prone to losing our attention we can also begin to explore ways to help us regain it and choose where we would like to direct it. Mindfulness teaches us that our attention is flexible and that it can be redirected to other aspects of our moment-to-moment experience. This means that with practice we can also begin to notice neutral as well pleasant inner experiences such as thoughts and feelings rather than being stuck rigidly in our own pain all the time. Knowing that we have this ability can be immensely helpful.

Following are four qualities or stages of attention. These qualities are also illustrated in Figure 6-1.

▶ **Gathering:** This in many ways is a subtle process, almost like collecting our focus, which might be scattered in some way. We can also say that in many ways this is the stage of collecting our effort or intention. We can use an example of when soccer players are about to kick a ball into the goalpost. Before they can actually go ahead and kick the ball into the net, they first of all need to gather their attention from where it was to the present moment; otherwise, they will not be able to focus on the task at hand.

In mindfulness practice, there is the simple stage of relaxing, settling in and noticing where our attention is right at this moment. So if our attention is lost on autopilot, we can simply acknowledge that and gather it in this way before we choose to then direct it to our body or to any of the five physical senses.

▶ **Directing:** This stage involves choosing an object to which we can direct our attention. For the soccer player this usually means directing the ball to the opponent's goalpost so that he or she can score a goal.

In mindfulness practice this means that once we have gathered our attention we can then choose where to direct it. In order for us to be able to direct our attention we have to have an object or anchor of attention, such as our feet or the breath, for example, or another place in the body where we can focus.

▶ **Keeping or maintaining:** Once we have gathered and directed our attention at a desired object, we then need to be able to hold and rest that attention or in some way keep the focus in a relaxed but sustained way. For the soccer players, this means that they need to be able to keep their attention on the goalpost and then kick the ball in a calculated way rather than being distracted by their own thoughts so that they can score the goal. As we know, they don't always get it right.

As we begin to explore mindfulness practice, we realise that our mind takes us places, and that it's not that easy to rest our attention on a specific chosen point such as the breath, our feet or any of the five physical senses. The mind wanders, but the practice is to train our mind

Part II: A Journey into Healing with Mindfulness

to be able to hold our attention on a specific point and as it wanders away we then redirect it back to the chosen point.

✓ **Shifting or redirecting:** This stage or component of attention simply means that we choose to redirect our attention if it gets lost. Not only that, but we can also choose to switch from focusing on one thing to focusing on another thing. So, for the soccer players, each time they lose focus thinking about other stuff they simply redirect their attention to the goalpost where they are aiming the ball.

As far as our mindfulness practice is concerned, this means that each time our mind gets lost and we lose our attention, we can acknowledge this and choose to bring it back to the chosen object of attention such as the breath. All of this is done with kindness and compassion. Having said this, our attention doesn't have to get lost. It can, for example, be resting on the breath, and then we can decide to simply shift it to another part of our body or another experience.

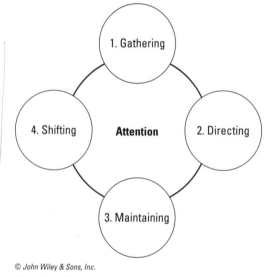

© John Wiley & Sons, Inc.

Figure 6-1: The four stages of cultivating attention.

Where attention goes, there energy flows

This basically means that the more attention you give to your unhelpful automatic habits and the negative thoughts they feed, the more depressed you will potentially become. The autopilot quality of mind keeps these negative thoughts active, and we know that these unhelpful negative thoughts lead to unpleasant feelings and low mood.

Following are some of the negative thoughts that often are fed by being on autopilot:

- ✔ I am a failure, and I will never be happy again.
- ✔ I am unlovable and will never find someone to love me.
- ✔ I will never recover from this and will always be unhappy.

It is okay to have these types of thoughts; most people have this constant inner-mind chatter going on all the time. People who are depressed, however, have such thoughts more often and more intensely. It is also worth remembering that these thoughts happen automatically and unconsciously, hence making it a challenge to be aware that they are there in the first place.

On the other hand, if you can begin to notice when you are on autopilot and begin to acknowledge this and bring your mind back to the five physical senses, you can begin to be more aware of what is going on in your own mind and choose to direct your attention away from such thoughts to more helpful and positive ones.

Decoding the Layers of Experience

The experience of depression is made up of many different layers. What we call a bad, crappy, low-mood feeling in the morning, for example, is composed of many aspects or layers of experience. It might come across as simply low mood or feeling like crap, but in actual fact there are many other aspects to this low mood.

Seeing depression through these different layers can help you find greater clarity and enable you to slowly see that your condition is not just one enormous unmanageable and over-powering experience. Rather, you can see a collection of little layers of experience that you can get to know, understand, befriend and learn to manage more skilfully and effectively.

We can say that there are at least five different layers which make up an experience. All these following layers (illustrated in Figure 6-1) are connected and dependent on each other. The first three are reasonably easy to spot where as the rest are definitely more unconscious and can be quite challenging to identify.

- **Thoughts:** In depression these are usually pessimistic and negative such as 'I am a bad person' or 'I am unlovable'. These negative thoughts then contribute and lead to uncomfortable feelings.

- **Feelings:** Feeling bad or low in some way is usually the first thing that we can be aware of. These feelings can be dense, heavy and deeply painful. At times, people feel numb and are unable to tell what they are feeling.

- **Sensations:** These are experienced more in the body as physical sensations such as tiredness, tension, pain or discomfort. People with depression often struggle with physical discomfort which doctors often call *psychosomatic*, or pain that does not have a diagnosable physical cause.

- **Memories:** Forgotten painful memories can often trigger uncomfortable feelings and thoughts, leading to a vicious cycle of depression. People with depression often say that they are stuck in painful memories which can keep the depression active.

- **Core beliefs:** These are all the negative unconscious belief patterns that have formed in the subconscious mind over the years, such as a strong embedded belief that you are somehow a bad person. This layer is what feeds the negative, unhelpful thoughts.

- **Generic mental patterns:** This aspect of experience is quite fundamental and is the same for all people. The core beliefs can be very unique and individual. For example, the automatic pilot quality of mind belongs to this category as well as the past or future thinking tendency.

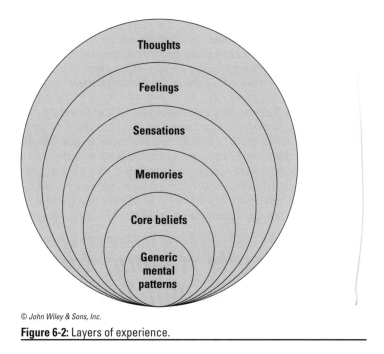

© John Wiley & Sons, Inc.

Figure 6-2: Layers of experience.

Say you wake up in the morning feeling low. The first thing you might notice is how bad you are feeling, and you might or might not be aware of any of the other layers. This is normal and totally okay. As I already mentioned, these layers are dependent on each other, which means that if you have a painful feeling you might then have a negative thought that goes with that feeling. With that there is usually a corresponding uncomfortable sensation in your body, such as tension or tiredness. Most people are, to some degree, aware of these three layers of experience. Looking even deeper at these layers you can also say that there are past memories associated with this experience. In other words, you might wake up feeling low and immediately connect this feeling with a past experience of feeling low yesterday. This will set off a whole chain reaction that leads to further thoughts of fear and resistance, which makes your mood deteriorate even further. Going a little deeper you might notice core beliefs that you may not even know you are believing such as 'I am weak' or 'I am unlovable' or 'I am stupid because I am depressed' and so on. We all have our personal ones. The last layer of the experience is made up of the generic mental patterns such as thinking excessively about the past or being lost on autopilot.

Another way of putting it is that depression can often feel like a big, heavy cloud you cannot see the end of, nor can you see the clear horizon. Mindfulness helps you to see that this cloud is made from smaller clouds which then bind together over time. These little clouds are all the layers of experience.

Mindfulness practice helps you to find a resting place, an anchor, where you can bring your attention away from these overwhelmingly uncomfortable experiences. Mindfulness doesn't push those experiences away or suppress them, but it allows you to simply acknowledge what is going on and return your attention to the five physical senses. In this way, you are less stuck in your head and more in a neutral place within your body. This is the foundation of mindfulness practice.

Yesterday Is History, Tomorrow Is a Mystery, But Today Is a Gift

Most of us are stuck on autopilot, and we don't even know it. This applies to people who are well and happy as well as those who are suffering from depression. Another very strong mental habit that we can get totally lost in is ***past and future thinking***. We all swing from either being stuck in the past, recalling painful memories, or planning excessively and frantically for the future (see Figure 6-3).

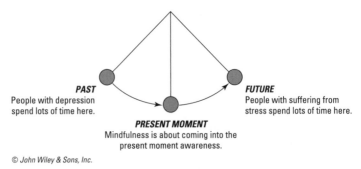

PAST
People with depression spend lots of time here.

FUTURE
People with suffering from stress spend lots of time here.

PRESENT MOMENT
Mindfulness is about coming into the present moment awareness.

© John Wiley & Sons, Inc.

Figure 6-3: Past, present and future thinking.

This way of being does have its benefits, so I am not saying that being this way is totally wrong. Thinking positively about the future is extremely helpful, for example, as it helps us to plan and create the life we would like to have. Having said this, we can get lost in this quality of mind, and being stuck in this habit robs us of our ability to live our life more fully in the present moment.

Another reason why thinking too much about the bad stuff that happened in the past is not good for us is that it contributes to negative rumination and negative self-talk, which makes depression worse.

We can say the same to thinking negatively and worrying about the future, where we have pessimistic-orientated thinking such as:

- ✔ My life will never be good and happy again.
- ✔ My future is dark and bleak.

When we suffer with depression we usually swing more excessively to past thinking and constantly recalling painful events. In many ways, we live our life stuck in the past. I'm sure you have experienced this just as I have, where you are in some way locked in as if in a prison of the past, constantly dwelling on either guilt or feeling wounded and hurt in some way:

- ✔ Guilty about things that we feel we have done wrong in the past
- ✔ Feeling hurt, wounded or angry at ourselves because someone else has hurt us in some way

Mindfulness practice helps us to notice this quality and rhythm of the mind, not by trying to get rid of it but by the simplicity of being aware of it. The more you are aware of this past/future tendency, the more you can bring your attention back to the present moment resting in the awareness of the five physical senses. Being this way will help you reduce your negative self-talk and empower you to live your life more fully and more happily.

To use the wisdom of the Kung Fu Panda, 'Yesterday is history, tomorrow is a mystery, but today is a gift – and that is why it is called a present'.

First and Second Arrow – Pain Is Inevitable, Suffering Is Optional

Often we react to our own thoughts and feelings, especially when they are uncomfortable or intense. We end up criticizing ourselves for having them in the first place. It's like it is not bad enough that we have the pain; now we have to put ourselves down for suffering as well.

In Buddhist psychology, we call this the *first and second arrow*. The first arrow is the initial pain, which in many ways is very generic and raw. This can be a painful thought or a deeply painful emotion or even an uncomfortable physical sensation or pain in the body.

The second arrow is the reactive self-judgment about it, such as, 'I am stupid because I have this problem'. In many ways this adds another layer of suffering to the already difficult situation, making us feel worse.

 The next time you notice that you are being overly self-critical for feeling or thinking in a particular way, simply notice this and see if you can give things permission to be as they are. You can even say to yourself, 'This is difficult for me right now, and I don't have to be perfectly happy. Hopefully, this will pass in time'.

Doing things this way will minimize the secondary suffering and help you reduce the intensity of the painful experience.

Thoughts Are Just Thoughts – They Are Not You

As you begin practising mindfulness, you will notice that your thoughts are not as solid as you might have first believed. You will also start noticing that you can shift your attention from one thought to another. In time, this will give you a greater feeling of freedom and ability to navigate through your own mental terrain and landscape. With practice, you will develop a greater sense of ease, as well as familiarity with your very own mind. Your thoughts and feelings will be less scary and more comfortable to look at. All this is possible with regular practice, patience and time.

One of the greatest benefits of mindfulness practice is that you will begin to notice that your thoughts are only that. They are not you; they are simply part of you. As you begin recognising this, you will be less inclined to believe everything that you think and will start relating to it from a much wiser position of being more of an observer rather than constantly getting entangled in the neverending stream of thoughts and mental images that so often pull and suck your energy.

Mindfulness teaches you to be the observer, allowing you to stand on the sidewalk of the busy highway of your own mind, where it a little safer. In this way you can watch the cars, your thoughts, pass by on the street in front of you. Your attention will get pulled, and you will be forced onto the street trying to interfere and direct the traffic. This is totally okay. With time you will learn that you can step back from the traffic of your own thoughts by pulling your attention back and allowing yourself to observe what is going on rather than be too involved in your own mental traffic.

This insight that you are not your thoughts is something that happens naturally and effortlessly through repeated practice. It cannot be hurried and artificially produced.

Chapter 7

Reconnecting with the Heart of Self-Compassion

Self-compassion, or the act of being kind to ourselves, is something that does not come easily for most people. Yet evidence strongly suggests that the practice of self-compassion does not only improve recovery from depression but also enhances our sense of wellbeing and happiness.

The struggle to cultivate and open a kind heart towards ourselves is shared by most people in modern society, and is not only limited to people affected by depression. Many people struggle with self-compassion because of a lack of nurture and parental love during childhood, but more so perhaps because as a society we place too much value on the intellect and not nearly enough value on cultivating a loving heart. Even though this struggle is common to us all, those of us living with depression often experience this lack of self-compassion more violently and more intensely than people who are not affected by the condition. The good news is that we can learn how to generate feelings of loving kindness and compassion towards ourselves.

What is self-compassion and what is the value of cultivating it? How can we begin to explore it in a real and authentic way for ourselves? Developing loving kindness through mindfulness is a progressive and gradual experience that can help us live well and it is through this chapter that I wish to invite you, if you care to, to explore this for yourself.

Exploring the Nature of Self-Compassion

Following is a traditional Zen story I encourage you to read:

> There once was an old woman whose job was to carry water up to the Zen meditation master so that he could cook food for himself. She did this freely and happily, and saw it as her way of practising meditation.
>
> The woman used buckets to carry the water. One of the buckets had a crack in it and always leaked water onto the sides of the path leading up to the Zen master's dwelling. The bucket felt so insufficient and bad, useless and deficient due to the fact that it could never deliver the whole bucket of water to the Zen master. At best it would deliver enough for a cup of tea.
>
> The cracked bucket continued feeling so bad and deficient and after many years of suffering in silence confessed this to the old woman.
>
> The woman said, 'Yes, well, I did notice that you had a crack on your side and leaked water, so I planted flower seeds which you then unknowingly watered'.
>
> 'Have you seen the flowers that are now blossoming on the sides of the path where you leaked the water?'
>
> The bucked replied, 'No I did not'. 'Well that's okay. Nonetheless, they are beautiful' said the woman. The bucket reflected on this and slowly started to change his view of himself.
>
> Our deficiency has beauty in it, and all we need to do is to acknowledge this. We all have aspects of ourselves that we find difficult to be with. We are all in some ways 'cracked buckets'.

In reading the story of the cracked bucket you might identify with how the cracked bucket felt, having struggled for so long in silence feeling afraid to tell the old wise woman about his deep sense of guilt and his overpowering feelings of inadequacy.

Personally, I first heard this story when I was a novice monk living in a Chinese Zen Buddhist monastery in South Africa; I was about 23 years old at that time and just beginning my meditation journey. After hearing the story I felt deeply moved in some strange way. It was as if I could see myself being that cracked bucket. I entered the monastery to help myself make sense of my confusion about my place in the world, and the very debilitating anxiety and depression that I was experiencing at that time. The story suggested something totally alien to me, and even though I was deeply moved by it, I struggled to truly experience its message. I felt quite a bit of resistance to the idea presented with this rather beautiful tale.

Looking back at it I now see that the reason I resonated with the story was because its message spoke directly to my heart, bypassing my head, and the reason why I struggled with it was because it suggested a crazy and radical idea: that I could somehow develop the capacity to feel okay with all my many faults, addictions, bad habits, unworthy aspects and flaws. As a result, the story continued to inspire me for years to come.

Refering back to the story earlier in the chapter, self-compassion is a lot like being the old wise woman who saw the situation from a different angle. She had wisdom, understanding and patience, and she responded to the bucket as such, offering it comfort, reassurance and the space for self-generated growth and insight.

Before we go on to explore the psychology and mechanics of compassion, I would like to that say self-compassion is definitely something we can purposefully choose to cultivate. Having a framework and a good psychological understanding is extremely helpful, but we can from the start remember that this is not something we can rush, think ourselves into or fabricate artificially. Self-compassion is something that we can experience, although very often, as in my case, it takes time and patience.

The nature of self-compassion is a softness and kindness of the heart we direct towards ourselves. It is very much like the warm sun that has been hidden from us behind the very heavy and dark clouds of depression. Even though we might not feel the sun, it is still there. The non-judgemental heart is always accessible to us.

Exploring Compassion and Self-Compassion

Having reflected on the story of the cracked bucket in the previous section, we can develop a certain underlying sense of the quality of compassion. However, we cannot leave things just there.

Before we can get to a point where we are able to understand and then practise self-compassion for ourselves, we need to understand the idea of compassion a little better.

Compassion can be approached from at least three different angles:

- ✔ The etymology or meaning of the word
- ✔ The psychology or the step-by-step process leading to the experience of compassion
- ✔ The neurochemistry of compassion or what happens in the brain when we feel kindness

The meaning of the word compassion

It's usually helpful to examine the etymology or the root meaning of any word related to a concept we are aiming to define. Doing this can often connect us with its original meaning.

The word *compassion* has its origins in the Latin language. The prefix *com-* means *with* and the *-passion* segment of the word roughly means *suffering*.

The prefix *com-* suggests that it has something to do with the quality of our relationship to suffering. In other words, how are we *with* our own the suffering as well as that of others?

When we see suffering, do we:

- ✔ Deny it or look away, saying it's not my problem
- ✔ Choose to look and acknowledge it and ask ourselves what could be done to alleviate it

The definition of compassion as being 'with suffering' is quite resonant with mindfulness. It indicates that it is only when we can see and acknowledge that suffering exists that we can try to help another in need.

The same applies to our own suffering. We can only be in a position to help ourselves when we can acknowledge our pain and with that at the same time have the wish for the suffering to ease and dissolve.

The psychology of compassion and self-compassion

Another way of looking at the idea of self-compassion is by acknowledging that you have different parts to your personality. Part of your personality is compassionate and understanding, but you also have a part of you that is more critical, impatient and lacking compassion. These parts develop as we grow older and interact with the world around us.

When you are depressed, the self-critical and judgemental part of your personality is much stronger than the kind and understanding aspect. For some of us, this is so much the case that we no longer feel we have any kindness or compassion left in us, neither for ourselves nor for anyone else either.

Compassion is the inherent human emotion that one feels in response to the suffering of others, and which motivates a desire to help. Put it in a different way, compassion is allowing ourselves to acknowledge and respond to the suffering we see in others.

Most of us find it easier to be kind and compassionate with our friends than we are with ourselves. For some reason we find it harder to have the same quality of mind for ourselves and yet we too are human. Self-compassion, however, encourages us to direct the same quality of heart towards our own experience.

I invite you to ask yourself these questions:

- ✔ What would you say to a friend who was in a similar situation to you?
- ✔ Would you be critical and demeaning or would you show understanding and patience?

In the next part of the chapter, I look at a step-by-step process of developing compassion.

The fact is that we do this automatically and don't really need to learn the skills to be able to be kind to our friend, but by breaking it into a step-by-step process it might be easier for us to then understand how we can apply the same process to our own situation and develop a similar sense of compassion towards ourselves.

For example, say that we have a friend in need and he just lost his job and would benefit from some support and kindness.

This process has three stages, namely: *noticing, resonating* and *responding*:

- ✔ **Noticing:** We need to notice and be able to acknowledge that our friend is suffering. In other words simply recognising that he is in pain and in need of some support.
- ✔ **Resonating:** We need to be somehow emotionally moved by his suffering so that we can resonate and perhaps identify and be able to understand what he might be going through. In other words by putting ourselves in his shoes we can get the sense of how difficult it must be for him.
- ✔ **Responding:** We need to be able to have a feeling of wishing for his suffering to dissolve so that he may feel better. In this way we can respond most appropriately in a skilful way by either offering some words of consolation or

giving advice or doing something that will be of benefit to his situation. We can also choose not to act and simply have the feeling of wishing him well and happiness.

Figure 7-1 shows the process leading up the point of being able to respond with compassion to a friend who might be in need.

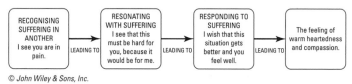

© John Wiley & Sons, Inc.

Figure 7-1: The three-step process of compassion.

Self-compassion is having the same quality of understanding and kindness that we have towards our friend but directed towards ourselves. We can follow a step-by-step process to develop the softness of heart towards our very own situation.

- ✔ **Noticing:** We can simply notice and acknowledge our difficulty rather than deny it or keep telling ourselves that we ought to be stronger or better in some way. In other words simply recognising that we are struggling and in need some support.

  We might even repeat this following phrase to ourselves:

  'I can see that this is hard for me, it is okay to feel like this, things are not easy right now'.

- ✔ **Resonating:** Here we can simply remind ourselves that this experience would be hard for anyone. We can even think what we would say to someone else who would be in our shoes. We are all human beings and you are no different from anyone else when it comes to feeling pain.

  You may wish to ask yourself:

  'How would I speak to my friend if he or she were in a similar situation to mine?'

- ✔ **Responding:** Here we can simply wish for ourselves for things to get better, to improve in some way. We can leave it with simply having a feeling or we can even take it a step further and take an action in the compassionate direction.

You may try saying the following phrase to yourself:

'I know that things are difficult for me, but I hope that I can find the strength and wisdom to find a way through it'.

The above might sound a bit complicated so simply try to recall the cracked bucket story at the beginning and remember that self-compassion is simply kindness directed towards yourself.

The neurochemistry of self-compassion

In Chapters 3 and 4, I explore the basic neuroscience behind mindfulness and also touch on the idea of the Reactive and Responding Mind as well as the corresponding brain networks and regions that get activated as a result.

In Chapters 4 and 5, you learn that qualities such as patience, mindful awareness and kindness all belong to the Responding Mind System and with that neurologically to the Task Positive Network part of the brain. Some of the brain regions that get activated when practising mindfulness are the: Prefrontal cortex, the insula and the hippocampus (shown in Figure 7-2).

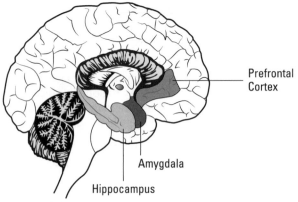

© John Wiley & Sons, Inc.

Figure 7-2: Parts of the brain activated during mindfulness meditation.

On the other hand we have the mental qualities such as fear, anxiety and self-criticism. These belong to the **Reactive Mind**

System, which neurologically corresponds to the Default Negative Network part of the brain with the amygdala region of the brain being overactive.

When we are stuck in self-criticism we keep the *amygdala* part of the brain switched on. The amygdala is the primitive part of the brain which is responsible for keeping us alert to danger. This is also the part of the brain that gets activated when we experience fear or the 'stress fight, flight or freeze' response. The amygdala signals other parts of the body to produce chemicals such as adrenaline and cortisol, which are again part of the stress response.

The constant state of self-criticism and judgement keeps the stress in our body response going, which often leads to making our depression worse.

Self-compassion, on the other hand, is a quality of mind belonging to the Responding Mind System. When we feel kindness for ourselves or for someone else, a tiny pea-sized part of the brain called the *pituitary gland* releases a naturally occurring brain chemical called *oxytocin* which plays a role in what is called the mammalian care-giving system. This mammalian system is what gets activated when a mother gives nurture and care to her child, for example.

One way that the care-giving system works is by triggering the release of oxytocin. Research now shows that an increase in this particular chemical strongly increases feelings of safety, trust, calm and warm-heartedness as well as our ability to feel a sense of warm-heartedness and compassion towards ourselves.

Oxytocin is also released when:

- ✔ We get a hug
- ✔ We are in tune with someone we like
- ✔ We play with a pet or a child

Research suggests that self-compassion may be a powerful trigger for the release of oxytocin. Knowing that there is a biological basis for self-compassion demonstrates the immense power of our own mind in changing our very own body physiology.

The Three Musketeers: Self-Esteem, Self-Confidence and Self-Compassion

There are three psychological qualities that are very useful to have in our lives. I call these the three musketeers. They are:

- ✔ Self-esteem
- ✔ Self-confidence
- ✔ Self-compassion

Having these in some way in our life can help us flow much more easily with the challenges of life. These three qualities also serve as protecting factors against depression. When we are depressed, however, it is most likely that we will lack the presence of all three in some way. This is totally understandable and okay and is part of having the condition.

There is a difference between self-esteem, self-confidence and self-compassion. They do, however, all have a particular function and in some way they all support each other just like the three musketeers do.

Research suggests that self-compassion is most helpful to people with depression as it can help people deal with often complex and challenging emotions such as guilt, shame and so forth that often accompany the condition of depression.

Self-esteem is to do with our own self-worth or how we feel and see ourselves as a person. Do we feel that we are an 'okay' or 'not okay' as a person? Do we feel worthy of attention and affection? These are just some of the emotional evaluations that decide whether we feel our image of ourselves is positive/balanced or negative/unbalanced and decide whether we have a healthy or unhealthy self-esteem.

Our level of self-esteem is often dependent on social norms or how we were treated by our parents as children and what we believe ourselves now to be. The limitation of self-esteem is that it is dependent on how we perceive ourselves rather than connecting with the fundamental universal reality of simply being a fragile human being.

Self-confidence is very much our view on our own abilities to do something, such as a specific task. Do we think we are good at playing tennis or doing maths, for example. The level of self-confidence is usually a result of overcoming certain obstacles or working to improve a skill. Succeeding in establishing these skills builds on our confidence. Our self-confidence is dependent on comparing ourselves to others or by matching it against certain self-created ideals.

We can have high self-confidence or be good at a particular task but have low self-esteem; in other words, we can feel unworthy as a person but still be very good at tennis. The reverse can also be true where we feel an 'okay' person inside but don't do well at tennis at all.

Self-compassion is connected to self-esteem and self-confidence, but at the same time in many ways it is independent of our ability to experience them. Self-compassion is more connected to the fundamental idea that you can have loving kindness towards yourself by the very fact that you are a human being. It is also connected to the universal truth that all human beings suffer, and it is because of that that you can feel entitled to feelings of warmth, understanding, patience, tolerance and compassion.

You can feel self-compassion even if:

- ✔ You do not feel good about yourself.
- ✔ You lack self-confidence and or self-esteem.
- ✔ You can feel your situation is unbearable or hopeless.
- ✔ You have feelings of guilt and or conflicting emotions.

Part of self-compassion is recognising our common humanity. In essence, understanding that everyone is flawed: this is part of the human condition. It helps to remember that you're not alone.

Research now shows that cultivating the quality of loving kindness can dramatically help us enhance our sense of emotional wellbeing.

Working with Resistance and Difficult Emotions Mindfully

We can from the start try to remember that cultivating self-compassion will be a process of discovery and often for many it takes time, continuous practice and patience.

When I started exploring self-compassion for myself I found that there was a lot of resistance that was coming to the surface as a result of the practice of self-kindness. I often felt that I didn't deserve to feel compassion for myself, as if there werer a major block to feeling this kindness of heart directed at my own mind and my own life. This is totally normal and part of the process of practising self-compassion. We don't have to try to get rid of the resistance or try to sort it out. Simply acknowledge it and say hello; in a way turn your attention towards it and give it space to be just the way it is. This is the mindful way of approaching any emotional blocks that you might encounter on your journey to self-compassion.

We make the resistance part of our practice and do not try to avoid it or give into and succumb to it. Here we can apply the mindful art of befriending our difficult emotions and even more radically we can offer that part warmth and compassion. Practising like this takes time but with a continued effort we can begin to transform the resistance and reduce its intensity.

 Rather than aiming not to have resistance, simply try to identify the resistance and name it. Perhaps even give it a shape or a colour, noticing what it looks like. Developing familiarity with this state can often help us reduce its intensity. Try it if you like, and simply acknowledge the resistance and let it be.

Trying a Self-Compassion Meditation

One very simple thing we can begin to do is to simply reflect on anything that was perhaps useful to you in this chapter. Notice what stood out, what ideas resonated with you and simply take stock of things as they are.

You may also wish to try the following self-compassion meditation.

This simple and easy to do self-compassion exercise has three stages.

1. **First shake and then rub your hands together to generate some heat.**

2. **In a relaxed way, place the left hand on your heart area, then your right hand on top of your left as in Figure 7-3.**

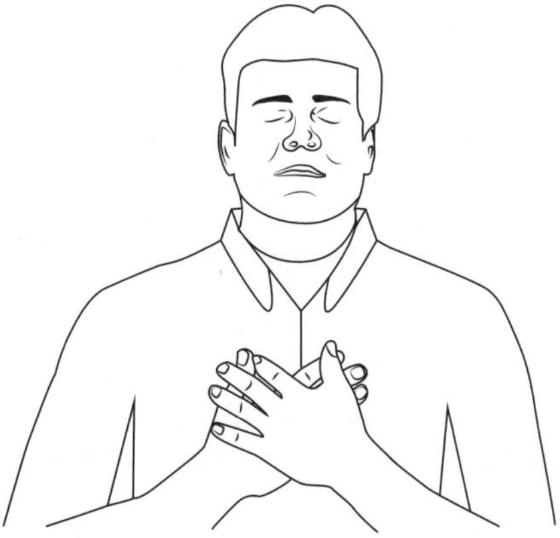

© *John Wiley & Sons, Inc.*

Figure 7-3: Self-compassion meditation hand posture.

Simply sense where your hands will be most comfortable. For some people it's directly over the heart. For others it's more in the centre of the chest. Simply take time to sense where you can feel most connected to your emotional heart centre using your touch.

3. **Now take a deep breath and relax into this posture and then place your attention to the area where your hands touch your chest.**

Notice the warmth of your own hands as they make contact with your heart. You may also bring in some gentle side-to-side movement with your hands, a kind of rocking sideways movement. Simply allow yourself to rest in this space for as long as you feel comfortable.

4. **Repeat the following phrases to yourself a few times, either silently or out loud. Don't worry if you can't connect with the words emotionally at first. Feeling the words can take some time and practice.**

> May I be free of suffering.
>
> May the depression begin to dissolve and ease.
>
> May I find the courage to heal.
>
> May I be well and happy.
>
> May I be peaceful and at ease.

5. **Let go of the practice. Take a few slow deep breaths and simply continue to sit for the next minute or so in silence, noticing what your experience is.**

Do not have any expectations, but simply notice what the effect, if any, of this exercise is. Take note, if you care to, of any particular thoughts or feelings that you became aware of, perhaps resistance or enjoyment, or something else totally unique to you.

It is very helpful when beginning to explore self-compassion for ourselves to go slowly and not aim to try to get rid of the inner critic or judge. Instead, give it space and allow it to be as it is.

Part III

Living Mindfully and Connecting with Happiness

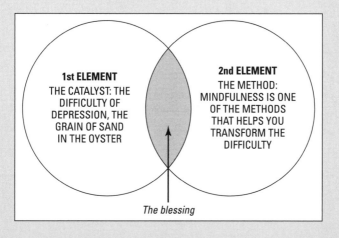

1st ELEMENT
THE CATALYST: THE DIFFICULTY OF DEPRESSION, THE GRAIN OF SAND IN THE OYSTER

2nd ELEMENT
THE METHOD: MINDFULNESS IS ONE OF THE METHODS THAT HELPS YOU TRANSFORM THE DIFFICULTY

The blessing

Head to www.dummies.com/extras/managing depressionwithmindfulness for a free article that discusses the uses and benefits of mindfulness practice, whether or not you're dealing with depression.

In this part . . .

- ✔ Try your hand at some easy-to-follow mindfulness exercises.

- ✔ Discover how to find the blessing in any difficulty.

- ✔ Get the lowdown on nine mindful attitudes and explore the difference between having a bad day and a bad life.

- ✔ Find out what taking the next step in your own journey to healing and recovery could mean to you.

Chapter 8

Five-Minute Mindfulness Practices

*U*nderstanding the basic theory and concepts behind mindfulness is just part of learning about it. Next, we put it into practice. Mindfulness can't just be about the theory: it's an experience, and it is not until we begin to explore its practical aspect that we begin to reap the benefit.

Those of us who suffer with depression know that trying to sit quietly can be incredibly challenging. This is mainly because it is not enjoyable to sit with your own uncomfortable mental experiences and low mood. This is quite normal. There is, however, a soothing, helpful and even enjoyable way we can begin to engage in the mindfulness exercise.

In this chapter, we will explore three short and effective mindfulness exercises that you can begin to practise straightaway. I guide you through the meditation postures as well the exercises which can be done sitting, lying or whilst moving your body. I invite you to explore what works best for you based on your energy levels, mood and personal preference.

If you are experiencing severe or clinical depression, contact your chosen health professional before doing any of the mindfulness exercises, as mindfulness can potentially make your condition worse.

Discovering Your Own Way

We are all individuals with uniquely different experiences, needs and personalities. What works for one person may not work for another. Take your time and explore what mindfulness exercises work best for you. You may resonate with some of the practices but not with others; you may find some exercises more helpful than others. You need to start somewhere, so just choose one that you feel may work for you and simply try it out. In time it may be a good idea to invest in a mindfulness audio CD as this is the easiest way of practising.

 The important thing is not so much what exercise you do but rather that you simply try it and notice the effects. This is an exploration rather than a competition.

Remind yourself constantly that doing the exercises is not about success or failure but rather about noticing what the experience is. If doing the exercise felt difficult then you can let that be that. If, on the other hand, you found the exercise easy and or enjoyable then you can notice that as well. Most of the time it will be a mixture of experiences and at times you will find it easy and at other times challenging.

 Just because you find the exercise challenging does not mean that you have failed in some way. Learning mindfulness is a process of discovery.

Things to Consider before Doing a Mindfulness Exercise

How do you choose what mindfulness exercise to do? One thing that may help you decide is to ask yourself what you need right now. The basic idea is to begin to sense what would be most helpful to you and your unique personal situation.

Choosing the most suitable exercise for you

Can you sense what your body is communicating to you?

- ✔ Would you benefit from some movement meditation?
- ✔ Do you feel a bit anxious and would it be best to do some sitting or lying down meditation practice?
- ✔ Maybe you feel tired and could do with mindful walk instead.
- ✔ Perhaps you would enjoy some music enjoyment meditation.

Simply tune into yourself and ask yourself out loud or silently 'What do I need right now? What exercises would suit me best right now?'

Creating a safe and supportive space

Creating a nurturing space where you can just be present with yourself and let things be is immensely helpful as it supports you in giving yourself permission to simply focus on healing and getting well.

- ✔ Can you set aside some quality time for yourself?
- ✔ Do you have access to a suitable safe space where you will not be disturbed by noises or daily responsibilities?

Create a mindful space in your house where you do your regular practice. It can be in your bedroom or sitting room, preferably away from any distractions such as television. The idea is to start associating the chosen place with calm and self-nurture. You may even want to try a few different areas of your house before you find the right spot. Take your time to explore this.

Choosing the best time

It is most effective to have a daily set time for the formal practice, this can be in the:

- ✔ Morning
- ✔ Afternoon
- ✔ When you wind down in the evening

The thing to consider is to check what would be the most appropriate time and also notice when you will be most alert and responsive to the exercise.

 It is not a good idea to do the lying down or sitting mindfulness exercise when you are physically tired as you may end up falling asleep. In this case, you may be better off doing a mindful movement exercise instead. Simply check in with yourself and take time to experiment and notice the effects of the practice; be gentle with lots of self-kindness.

Your informal practice of taking a deep breath can take place anywhere and anytime as long as you can remember to catch yourself to do it.

This can be when you are:

- ✔ Driving by staying focused on the process of driving itself and noticing things around you
- ✔ Sitting on the bus or train
- ✔ Waiting in the bank queue or post office feeling flustered

Step-by-step preparation

Before we begin to explore the actual guided mindfulness exercises it is a good idea to get to know that there is a process involved. By understanding the process more clearly you will hopefully find the experience helpful.

All in all there are five basic steps for completing mindfulness exercises:

1. **Decide what exercise you will be exploring.**

   Select an exercise mentioned in this chapter. Choose a meditation that you feel will be most helpful to you and your situation. If you don't know what would be most helpful then that's okay too. You are more than welcome to try any one of the exercises in this chapter. The point to remember is that this is an exploration and not about getting it right in any way whatsoever.

2. **Create a safe space.**

   As we explored in the prior section, see if you can find a space where you will be undisturbed, feeling safe enough to let go and take care of yourself. Make sure that your phone is switched off.

3. **Read through the exercise a few times.**

   Part of this exercise is to get a sense of the technique, so rereading the text a few times may be helpful. Each exercise has three easy steps and becoming more familiar with the process involved will help you relax into it more. Remember that it may potentially take a few times for you to begin to flow more easily with the exercise. In some ways it's like learning to ride a bike: it gets easier with practice and time.

4. **Just do it.**

   Once you have decided what the practice is going to be and where you will be doing it and you have read through the text then you may want to just do it.

   You can keep the page open on the exercise but the easiest way is to simply remember the main points to the exercise and don't worry about getting it right: just do what you remember

5. **Reflect on how it was for you.**

   Once you have completed the exercise, it is very helpful to reflect how the experience was for you. Following are some questions you may ask yourself:

   • Did you feel it was easy, hard, or somewhere in the middle?

- Was it enjoyable, not enjoyable or something completely different?
- What thoughts crossed your mind?
- What emotions arose for you?

It's an idea to keep a diary of your reflections. Each time you complete an exercise, simply write down anything that you noticed in terms of your experience, without analysing it in any way.

Three Types of Posture: Sitting, Lying and Standing

The mindfulness exercises described this chapter will be done sitting, standing or lying down. It is important to have a good understanding of the correct posture as this will:

- ✔ Help you get the most out of the mindfulness exercise
- ✔ Prevent posture related injuries
- ✔ Support your ability to focus and relax

Research shows that having a certain posture can actually help us switch on certain parts of the brain associated with attention, focus and relaxation. So it's worth developing at least a basic understanding of the basic postures.

The sitting posture

The siting posture is a very stable one and can support you in cultivating a sense of awareness. The benefits of sitting up rather than lying down are:

- ✔ It reduces sleepiness and the risk of nodding off.
- ✔ Helps you with good back posture.
- ✔ Brings back a sense of confidence.

It is important that you sit using a hard chair or a chair that is not overpadded, like a sofa chair, for example. The idea is to sit on the edge of the chair with your feet making contact with the floor, resting the heels and toes flat on the floor surface.

Let me now go through the sitting posture guidelines:

1. **Allow your head to simply relax into the top of your spine making sure that your head is straight and not tilted to either side.**

2. **Slightly tuck in your chin and simply relax.**

3. **Allow your shoulders to drop and relax.**

   Simply feel yourself sitting with a sense of dignity and natural confidence.

4. **Sit with your buttocks and pelvis resting on the chair making full contact with the surface. Then just ever so slightly push out your lower belly and lean forwards a few degrees.**

5. **Sit with your eyes closed or open – either is fine.**

   If you are leaving your eyes open then simply lower your gaze on the floor as if looking on the ground about a meter away from you and lower your eyelids slightly.

6. **Rest your hands palms up or down on your thighs or wherever you feel most comfortable.**

7. **Allow yourself to sense the force of gravity pulling your body into the chair.**

Figure 8-1a demonstrates an incorrect posture. You can see the person slumping forwards, which often contributes to low energy and fatigue. Figure 8-1b shows the correct meditation posture with the spine straight but relaxed.

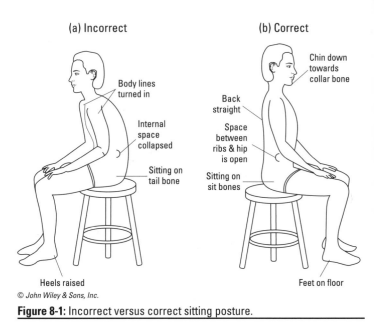

(a) Incorrect

Body lines turned in

Internal space collapsed

Sitting on tail bone

Heels raised

(b) Correct

Chin down towards collar bone

Back straight

Space between ribs & hip is open

Sitting on sit bones

Feet on floor

© John Wiley & Sons, Inc.

Figure 8-1: Incorrect versus correct sitting posture.

The lying posture

The lying posture is another alternative you can explore. This posture helps you to create a space where you can feel comfortable and secure. Use this posture if sitting up is too difficult, or if you have spinal problems or other related physical conditions.

Following are the benefits of this particular meditation posture:

✔ It helps you to reduce physical pain by allowing your body to be thoroughly supported by the floor or by your bed.

✔ It helps you to relax into your body.

✔ Is excellent for your spine if you struggle to sit up straight in a chair.

Simply lie down on your bed or, if you notice that you fall asleep whilst doing a meditation practice on your bed, put a blanket on the floor and lay on top of that. Use a pillow to support your head and knees, as shown in Figure 8-2. You can also put pillows under your elbows. Allow your arms to rest on the sides of your body with palms up or down or alternatively rest your hands on your belly. Try to keep your legs uncrossed. Allow yourself to simply relax in to this support.

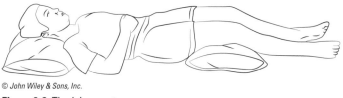

© John Wiley & Sons, Inc.

Figure 8-2: The lying posture.

The standing posture

The standing meditation posture is usually reserved for mindful movement meditation. You can carry out the exercises whilst standing if you feel your mind is particularly wandering or if your physical energy is low and you feel tired. Doing so will help you stay awake and help you be more aware of the five physical senses.

The main benefit of the standing posture is that it helps to ground your awareness in the body and away from your chattering mind.

Follow these steps to achieve the correct standing position:

1. **Spread your feet about shoulder width apart and turn your feet slightly inwards so that they are parallel rather than turning outwards.**

2. **Keep your back straight and relaxed and allow your shoulders to drop and relax.**

3. **Allow your head to simply rest on the top of your spine, keeping it straight and at ease.**

4. **Let your arms hang loosely at your sides.**

5. **Bend your knees slightly, as shown in the Figure 8-3a and b, and let the weight of your body be supported by your knees as well as the entire skeleton structure.**

   Figure 8-3c shows the incorrect way of standing and needs to be avaoided.

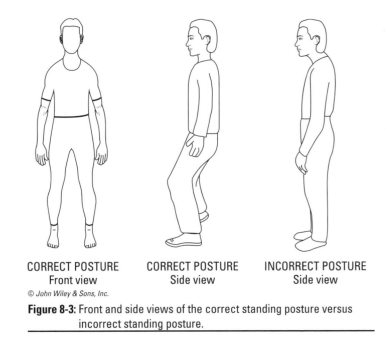

CORRECT POSTURE
Front view

CORRECT POSTURE
Side view

INCORRECT POSTURE
Side view

© John Wiley & Sons, Inc.

Figure 8-3: Front and side views of the correct standing posture versus incorrect standing posture.

Five-Minute Breath Meditation

This exercise is a good beginner's practice. You can use it when you need to centre and calm your mind. You can use this exercise on its own or combine it with any of the other practices in this chapter.

Note: This exercise is best done sitting up. You may, however, also do it lying down if you prefer.

Doing the exercise

The aim of exercise is to simply begin working with your breath. The idea is to take a few deep breaths, allow the breathing to adjust and settle and then simply notice what the quality of your breath is.

Follow these steps to complete this simple breathing exercise:

1. **Adopt a sitting posture and double-check that you are sitting comfortably.**

   Refer to the sitting posture guidelines earlier in the chapter if needed.

2. **Begin to take a few conscious slow and deep breaths.**

   You don't need to breathe any particular way. Your breaths should just be slower and deeper.

3. **Allow your body to relax with each exhalation. Don't force the exhalation but simply allow the breath to leave your body effortlessly and naturally. Drop and relax your shoulders with each natural exhalation.**

   You may want to limit the amount of deep breaths to about five. Make sure you keep the breath slow yet comfortable.

   You may notice that after taking a few deeper breaths your breathing will adjust and then develop its own natural rhythm.

4. **After taking a few conscious breaths, let go so that your body can take over the breathing again.**

5. **At this point you may still be tempted to control your breath, but as best you can, let go and give it back to your body.**

6. **Give yourself plenty of time and allow the breath to adjust itself to the level best for your body.**

   Don't try to control this process. Let your body do it for you.

7. **Take some time to discover the rhythm of your breath.**

8. **For the next minute or so, simply rest your attention on the natural flow of the breath.**

9. **Check where in your body you can feel the in and the out breath.**

   In other words, where in your body can you sense the breath the strongest? Is it at the tip of your nose? The chest or the lower abdomen? Or maybe somewhere else completely?

10. **Now simply notice the quality of your breath.**

   Is it fast or slow? Deep or shallow? Rough or smooth? Comfortable or uncomfortable? Or something unique to you?

   You may have thoughts, feelings and other bodily sensations coming in and out of your awareness, and you may even get lost in them. This is totally normal and okay. Simply notice it all with a kind and gentle attention and return your attention to exploring the quality of your breath and bring it back to the point in your body where you can sense the breath the strongest.

11. **When you feel ready, simply open your eyes (if they were closed) and bring your attention back to full waking consciousness.**

Relax and don't try too hard. This exercise is not about getting it right or wrong, but simply an opportunity to begin to explore how you can use your breath to affect your state of mind and mood. It's all about learning from your experience.

How was it for you? Reflecting on the exercise

Once you have completed the exercise it is very helpful to reflect how the experience was for you.

Some of the questions you may want to ask yourself are:

- ✔ Was it easy, difficult or something different?
- ✔ Did you notice any thoughts, feelings, memories and or sensations? Do not analyse, simply notice.
- ✔ What was the quality of your breath?
- ✔ Anything else that you may have noticed?

Five-Minute Mood Enhancer Meditation

This exercise is best done standing up and is particularly good if your energy or mood is low and you feel that you may benefit from some mindful movement.

Note: You normally do this exercise with your eyes closed, but you may want to leave them open if you prefer.

Doing the exercise

The aim of the exercise is twofold:

- ✔ To help raise your physical energy
- ✔ To bring your attention back from being stuck on uncomfortable thoughts and/or depressing feelings

Follow these steps to complete this mood enhancer meditation:

1. **Adopt a relaxed and comfortable standing posture.**

   Refer to the standing posture guidelines earlier in the chapter if necessary.

2. **Begin to take a few conscious slow and deep breaths.**

   You don't need to breathe any particular way. Your breaths should just be slower and deeper.

3. **Allow your breathing to settle and give your breath back to your body as described in the Five-Minute Breath Meditation.**

4. **Allow yourself to notice how you are standing, being particularly aware of where your feet are making contact with the floor.**

   Simply rest in this posture for the next few moments.

5. **On the next in-breath raise both arms so that they are horizontal, hands loose and palms facing downward. On the out-breath lower both arms to your side. See Figure 8-4.**

   Repeat slowly ten times, keeping your upward hand movement synchronised with your in-breath and the downwards movement with the out-breath.

   You may also bend your knees a little on the exhalation and straighten them out on the inhalation.

6. **Allow yourself to notice what you sense in your legs, feet, arms, hands and your body in general.**

   If your mind wanders, that's perfectly normal. Simply acknowledge it and with kindness bring it back to focusing on your movements.

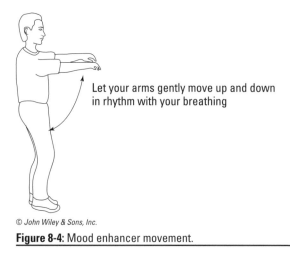

Let your arms gently move up and down in rhythm with your breathing

© John Wiley & Sons, Inc.

Figure 8-4: Mood enhancer movement.

7. **After about ten movements simply bring yourself to stillness. With your knees still bent a little, your arms resting at your side and with your eyes closed, simply rest in the awareness of what you sense in your body.**

8. **Notice any new sensations, any changes in your energy and mood levels.**

   Stay in this posture for the next minute or so or until you feel comfortable enough to end the exercise.

9. **Open your eyes and simply give your body a good shake. Bring your attention back to full waking consciousness.**

How was it for you? Reflecting on the exercise

Once you have completed the exercise once again reflect how the experience was for you.

Some of the questions you may want to ask yourself are:

- ✔ Was it easy, difficult or something different?

- ✔ Did you notice any thoughts, feelings, memories or sensations? Do not analyse; simply notice.

> ✔ What was the quality of your breath?
>
> ✔ Did you notice any changes in the quality of your energy or mood?
>
> ✔ Did you notice anything else?

Five-Minute Music Enjoyment Meditation

This music enjoyment mindfulness exercise is best done lying down on a blanket on the floor or on your bed.

Note: You usually do this exercise with your eyes closed, but you may leave them open if you prefer.

Doing the exercise

The aim of the exercise is explore your sense of sound and bring about feelings of enjoyment through the appreciation of your favourite music.

Follow these steps to complete this music enjoyment exercise:

1. **Choose a favourite piece of music.**

   Try to choose music that is relaxing in some way and that does not have too much beat in it. Choose one or two tracks. Use earphones if you want, or simply play the music through your speakers. Make sure that you adjust the volume so that it's not too loud.

2. **Switch on the music and let it play in the background.**

3. **Adopt a relaxed and comfortable lying down posture.**

   Refer to the lying posture guidelines earlier in the chapter if necessary.

4. **Begin to take a few conscious slow and deep breaths.**

   You don't need to breathe any particular way. Your breaths should just be slower and deeper.

5. **Allow your breathing to settle, and give your breath back to your body.**

   Try not to control your breathing; just let it happen.

6. **Relax your shoulders and the rest of your body on each exhalation.**

7. **Give yourself plenty of time and allow the breath to adjust itself to the level best for your body.**

   Don't try to control this process. Let your body do it for you.

8. **Take some time to discover the rhythm of your breath.**

9. **For the next minute or so simply rest your attention on the natural flow of the breath.**

10. **Simply notice the quality of your breath.**

    Is it fast or slow? Deep or shallow? Rough or smooth? Comfortable or uncomfortable? Or something uniquely different to you?

11. **Now begin to slowly shift your attention from noticing the quality of the breath to the sound of the music.**

    Let your focus rest on the sound itself. Each time your mind drifts off, allow it to. Just let it drift off and then gently but firmly bring it back to noticing the sound of the music.

12. **Allow yourself to appreciate the music and simply notice the different aspects of it, such as the rhythm, the pitch, the loudness and so on.**

    See if you can remain curious about the variety of the experience.

13. **You may have certain thoughts, feelings and memories arise, and that is perfectly okay. Simply acknowledge them and let them be. Reinvite your attention to the sound of the music itself. Let your attention continue to rest on the sound itself.**

    Do this over and over again or as many times as you like. Be playful and have a curious attitude towards the experience.

14. **After the music stops simply notice your experience and spend some time in this state of mind.**

15. **When you are ready simply open your eyes and bring your attention back to full waking consciousness.**

How was it for you? Reflecting on the exercise

Once you have completed the exercise once again reflect how the experience was for you.

Some of the questions you may want to ask yourself are:

- ✔ Was it easy, difficult or something different?
- ✔ Did you notice any thoughts, feelings, memories or sensations? Do not analyse; simply notice.
- ✔ Did you notice any changes in the quality of your energy or mood?
- ✔ Did you notice anything else?

Chapter 9

Discovering the Blessing within Depression

In This Chapter

▶ Learn how you can begin to move beyond depression

▶ Use your experience of struggle to help others

▶ Discover the benefits of finding your higher purpose

Character cannot be developed in ease and quiet. Only through experience of trial and suffering can the soul be strengthened, ambition inspired and success achieved.

–Helen Adams Keller

*P*art of the healing journey to wellbeing is to encourage yourself to explore a deeper meaning within your experience of depression. In other words, you explore the possibility that there is some good in your difficult situation, or that something good can come out of it.

Practising mindfulness can support you to see some value in the way things are right now. By looking for something of value and meaning in a seemingly meaningless situation you can begin to see your own suffering not as a curse but rather as an opportunity for growth and personal transformation.

As strange as this may seem, people who practise mindfulness often report feeling grateful toward their difficulties. It is that very difficulty which has been the catalyst needed to help them cultivate a sense of compassion for themselves and others as well as a deeper appreciation for the simple fact of being alive.

It really is possible that by practising mindfulness you can begin to see the blessing in your situation. This is quite a radical idea, I know, but it's true. Seeing your seemingly mean-ingless and negative situation as a potential blessing in dis-guise is exactly what is going to help you move beyond your chronic unhappiness and support in regaining your sense of wellbeing. I invite you to explore this for yourself in a way that works best for you.

Making Pearls: Gaining Strength from Your Depression

When you are feeling depressed, your own view of what is possible is very bleak and distorted. You can have a strong negative conviction that your life is very much useless and pointless. There is a sense of loss of personal meaning, as if you don't matter anymore, and you often feel as if you can be of no value to anyone.

To help people challenge this deep-seated conviction that their suffering is pointless and without any meaning, I often use metaphors. Metaphors are phrases or stories which are symbolic of a psychological idea that can be of great help when recovering from depression. The metaphor that I would like to use in this chapter is one relating to making precious pearls.

A pearl is made when a grain of irritating sand enters the inside of an oyster. The sand gets stuck between the inner membrane of the shellfish. In an attempt to free itself from the grain of sand which has just invaded its space the oyster secretes and covers the intruder with a protective substance called a nacre, which is the same material as that of the shell. Over time these layers of nacre, also known as mother-of-pearl, coat the grain of sand until the beautiful pearl is formed.

This metaphor of a pearl really does relate to you and your situation, unlikely though that may seem. If you think about it, pearls are made when a severe form of irritation and pain is transformed into something precious, beautiful and valuable. It's almost as if the oyster is able to use this seemingly bad experience and transform it into something good.

You may think, 'Ah, you're pulling my leg. What does the oyster know about being depressed?' You are right. The oyster probably doesn't know much about depression (or anything else, for that matter) but there is a similarity between you and the oyster.

The oyster didn't ask to have the sand stuck in its shell. It was put on the spot, so to speak, and had find a way of dealing with the irritation. Your depression is similar. You didn't ask to be depressed, but for some reason you are. Depression puts you in the corner with nowhere to run. Here you have a choice, you can get resigned to the situation or you can begin to explore ways of healing through it mindfully.

The point of this metaphor is to encourage you to reflect on the possibility of moving beyond depression by looking for possible blessings in your seemingly hopeless situation. We explore this idea of a blessing in more detail in this chapter – so please stay tuned.

Making depression creative

Many famous people have suffered from depression. They have all managed to somehow use it to their advantage either in the movies they made or the songs or books they wrote. Following is a list of people you might recognise.

- Stephen Fry, British actor, presenter and activist

- Eric Clapton, British musician

- Bob Dylan, American singer-songwriter, poet and artist

- Frank Bruno, British boxer

- Ruby Wax, American comedienne

- Robbie Williams, British pop singer

- Sir Winston Churchill, British Prime Minister

- J. K. Rowling, British writer

Moving beyond Depression Is Possible

Research in neuroscience demonstrates that the brain changes and grows new neural connections all the time. This phenomenon is called *neuroplasticity*. What is more amazing is that scientists have discovered that when you practise mindfulness you can measure which specific areas of your brain involved in experiencing a sense of wellbeing grow in size and density as a result of your meditation practice. This proves that you can bring about positive change. What this also suggests is that even from a purely physical point of view happiness is possible.

It is okay not to believe that you will not be happy again. However, it might be helpful to remind yourself that just because you don't feel or believe in the possibility of regaining your sense of wellbeing right now, does not mean that it's impossible. With time, your views may change, and you will regain your sense of hope.

When you are depressed it can feel as if you have been downgraded and forced to take up a low-paying job that you don't enjoy. You may feel like you have become a lesser kind of person.

Once you reach out for help, start receiving the right support and begin to apply mindfulness, your life begins to heal and things change for the better.

Some of the positive changes can be:

- ✔ Your level of mood improves.
- ✔ You will sleep less during the day and have more energy.
- ✔ Your thoughts will be more balanced and more optimistic about your future.
- ✔ Your values and your sense of what is important to you might change.
- ✔ You will discover new exciting opportunities and blessings in your experience.

Your life might never be the same after you have been through depression, and by applying mindfulness to your journey of healing you may become a happier and more enriched person, almost as if you have been offered a better-paying job that you also enjoy a little bit more.

This new job can be a challenge, though: you don't really know what to expect – mainly because it is new – and you are not used to it.

This transition from depression to feeling well takes time, as well as lots of courage and patience on your part. You need to go slowly and begin to get used to the new, more happy life. In the same way as it takes time when you switch jobs and have to learn what the new role demands of you. The same applies to moving beyond your condition.

Moving beyond depression does not mean that you will never feel down again or that you will not relapse. You may still have bad days, but if you are willing to develop the skills needed to manage your mood more effectively you will be able to enjoy a much happier life.

Moving beyond depression and into happiness means that you:

- ✔ Still experience depression but continue to find ways to manage your condition more effectively
- ✔ Try to learn to live well despite your condition
- ✔ Continue to learn how to shift your focus outward towards new positive and exciting possibilities
- ✔ Explore positive opportunities in which you can use your experience to help others in similar situations

Try to reflect what moving beyond depression could mean for you personally. How would your life be if you felt better? Who do you think you could be without the depression?

Moving beyond Depression: The Four Pillars of Happiness

As you start supporting yourself using the ideas and techniques in this book, you can naturally begin to move beyond depression and feel a greater sense of wellbeing.

There are four major principles that you can implement that will help you move beyond your depression and empower you to step into a greater sense of wellbeing. I call these the *four pillars of happiness.*

The four pillars are:

✔ Finding value and meaning in your experience, in other words looking for the blessing in disguise

✔ Creating the conditions for your happiness and wellbeing

✔ Understanding that your experience wasn't in vain and that you can, if you so choose to, be of service and benefit to others who might be going through a similar experience

✔ Connecting with your higher life purpose

These four pillars support you individually, but they also enhance each other as shown in the below diagram with the arrows pointing both away from each pillar (circle) as well as towards the next pillar. Each of these pillars also helps you directly to step into a new and potentially rewarding life filled with a new sense of direction and numerous positive possibilities, as represented by the picture of the happy person at the centre of Figure 9-1.

The following sections look at these four pillars of happiness in more detail.

The first pillar: Connecting with value and meaning

Believing that something good and of value could come of out a seemingly meaningless experience can dramatically enhance your chances of recovering from depression.

This view is supported by Viktor Frankl, MD, PhD, an Austrian neurologist, psychiatrist and Holocaust survivor.

Frankl devoted his life to studying and promoting meaning. He himself survived the Holocaust by finding personal meaning in the experience, which gave him the will to live through it. He went on to later establish a new school of existential therapy called *logotherapy*, based in the idea that man's underlying motivator in life is a will to find meaning, even in the most difficult of circumstances. Frankl observed that those prisoners who found some meaning in their deeply painful experience were more likely to survive the concentration camp than those who did not.

Looking for some kind of meaning, value or good in your situation can ultimately lead you to discover a blessing in disguise. It is helpful to remember that in order to find a blessing you first of all have to be willing to look for it or at least be willing to stay open to the idea that it's there.

Another way of looking at it is that when we have pain in the body we don't just ignore it. We attend to it because we know that it's the body's intelligent way of telling us that we need to attend to something, that something needs looking at. The same applies to depression where the mind is telling us that we need to look within and begin to ask ourselves what is it that we need to explore and get in touch with.

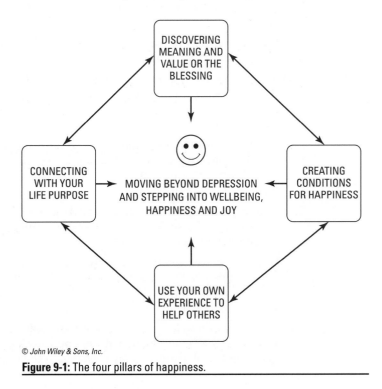

© John Wiley & Sons, Inc.

Figure 9-1: The four pillars of happiness.

It is possible that right now you perhaps feel unable or unwilling to see things in a more open or positive way and this is okay. Once you begin to practise mindfulness you will discover that your negative and unhelpful thoughts are not as solid and as real as you previously believed. In fact, you will discover that thoughts and feelings are just that – namely, passing aspects of your own mind and that you can choose what you think in ways that are more helpful and positive.

The following list outlines the possible value and blessings in depression: Depression does all the following:

- ✔ **It slows you down.** Depression can give you the opportunity and time needed to stop struggling, take stock, reflect on and process things.

- ✔ **It gives you a rest.** This rest protects you from the damage you might do to yourself from following a hectic lifestyle.

- ✔ **It is a catalyst in helping you develop compassion.** Depression can develop your capacity for compassion towards yourself and others.

- ✔ **It helps you accept true human vulnerability.** You begin to a see life for what it truly is – namely, very fragile.

- ✔ **It gives you the opportunity to develop wisdom through your own experience.** This can bring the realization that life is made of light and darkness, happiness and unhappiness.

- ✔ **It supports you in becoming more comfortable with the fact that suffering is part of life and is experienced by everybody.** After all, you have first-hand experience and a sense of familiarity with it.

- ✔ **It helps you to put things in perspective.** You will no longer sweat the small stuff and have a greater appreciation for what is really important in life.

- ✔ **It will empower you to have a greater sense of resilience.** Once you have been in the great abyss of depression and have survived it you know that you can deal with pretty much anything.

- ✔ **It enables you to learn and develop life skills that you would otherwise not have had the opportunity to gain.** In depression you are in many ways put in the corner with nowhere to run and you have to learn to either swim or drown.

✔ **It will make you a more real and authentic person.** Depression can help you move away from being purely materialistic and driven by money.

Getting something good or a blessing out of a seemingly meaningless and difficult situation depends on two key elements:

✔ **The depression itself:** The grain of sand in the oyster. This is the catalyst that is often needed for personal growth and improvement.

✔ **The method which gives us the ability to transform depression into a blessing:** In the example of the oyster it is its ability to secrete the nacre that then surrounds the grain of sand and overtime transforms it into a pearl.

In your situation, depression is the catalyst or difficulty, and mindfulness is the method that will help you find the blessing and support in moving forwards into a life of happiness.

The blessing or the something good is that which comes about as a result of the interaction between the two elements. Figure 9-2 shows how the two elements interact with each other; the area in the middle where the two circles superimpose on each other can be said to be the blessing.

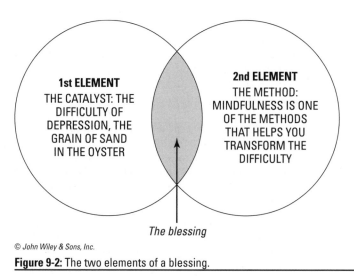

The blessing

© John Wiley & Sons, Inc.

Figure 9-2: The two elements of a blessing.

The second pillar: Creating the conditions for happiness

As you start applying mindfulness to your life, you will notice that you are able to make better choices that help you pave the path ahead to a greater sense of wellbeing and happiness. There are two aspects to creating the conditions for happiness, namely:

- ✔ Noticing positive things
- ✔ Making *therapeutic lifestyle changes* (TLCs) that help bring about happiness

These two aspects are like the two sides of the same coin; one helps the other. This means that you will find it easier to make actual positive changes and take part in enjoyable activities if you can first acknowledge the positives that are already in your life.

Noticing the positives in your life

It is human nature to constantly look for the negatives in our life and this quality is more prevalent with people who are depressed. Simply try and see if you can reverse the process and rather than scanning your life for the bad and negatives you choose to start acknowledging the positive in your life. Doing so will help you to make actual positive life changes.

You might notice that your mood is much lighter on one day than on another or that today you managed to leave the house. Sometimes you might feel that there isn't much positive in your life, in which case noticing that you are in less pain than on other days can also be encouraging and helpful.

You may want to experiment with keeping a positive diary where you note any positive aspects of your life. This can be as basic as noticing the fact that you have a house to live in with enough food to eat. Alternatively you can note any changes in your activities such as your mood level being better on one day than another.

Moving on and feeling happy: Making therapeutic lifestyle changes

Making therapeutic lifestyle changes (TLCs) simply means that you consciously choose to behave in ways that give you a sense of meaning, value and happiness. The term was developed by Roger N. Walsh, Professor of Psychiatry, Philosophy and Anthropology at the University of California Irvine. It suggests that you can bring about a sense of mental wellbeing by making specific positive changes in your day-to-day lifestyle.

When you feel unwell you probably don't feel like doing things that will make you feel better. In order to move beyond depression, however, you need to make the jump and begin to explore ways in which you can create conditions that will naturally help you to feel better and be happy.

Here are the eight TLCs that you can begin to explore:

- ✔ **Eating nutritious food:** Eat a healthy and varied diet which contains lots of vitamins and minerals necessary for good brain function.

- ✔ **Spending time in nature:** Get out of doors and in the natural world as much as possible. Fresh air and moderate sunshine are good for mental health.

- ✔ **Finding meaning in supportive relationships:** Spend time with friends and family. We are social beings and need to feel connected to others.

- ✔ **Spending time on recreation:** Have fun from time to time. Do something silly or go and see a movie if you can.

- ✔ **Relaxing and managing stress:** Mindfulness is a wonderful way of helping you to relax and manage your mood.

- ✔ **Taking exercise:** Mindful walking or any movement such as Yoga or Chi Kung is very beneficial, as it helps to release the naturally occurring happy chemicals called endorphins.

- ✔ **Experiencing spiritual involvement:** Explore prayer, dancing, meditation or anything that helps you get in touch with your higher human potential.

- ✔ **Offering service to others:** Explore various community wellbeing projects such as a walking group. Get involved in volunteering at a mental health charity, or start an online blog and share what has helped you cope on your journey, making it positive. This will help remind you of your own positive experience.

The third pillar: Using your experience of pain to help others

Another way to help support your recovery and chances of stepping into happiness is by using your own experience of hardship to help others. This is by far the greatest blessing in disguise.

People who have gone through deep pain and have come through the other side are an inspiration to others. They are a beacon of light and hope that others move towards. The reason why people are drawn towards such individuals is not because they have all the answers to their problems, but because those individuals have been where others may be now.

Choosing to be of service to others is a wonderful opportunity to use your own life as an instrument to benefit humanity. This means that by the very fact that you have suffered you will be of value to other people who might be struggling with similar difficulties.

One of the benefits of choosing to use your experience to benefit others is that it takes the focus away from yourself and at the same time gives you the opportunity to get involved in something greater than you and your problem.

Using your experience to help others is not the same as helping others so that you can just feel better about yourself. You can, however, choose to use your life experience as a means of helping others based on the understanding that it will not only enrich your own life but also that of those you touch. This idea is based on the principle that when you give with love you receive joy.

You can help others in small informal ways such as by sharing your story in a positive way. Why not try posting an online video on what has helped you in your recovery?

You don't need to be famous or free from depression in order to be of benefit to others. You simply need to be well enough and feel up to it and be interested in the idea.

Developing meaning from suffering

There is a beautiful real-life example of a man named Nick Vujicic. Nick, an Australian, was born with *tetra-amelia syndrome*, a rare disorder characterised by the absence of all four limbs. He tried committing suicide when a teenager by throwing himself in a pool of water hoping that he would drown. Somehow he pulled himself out and survived. He suffered severe depression due to his disability as he struggled to come to terms with his inevitable situation. Nick is now a motivational speaker educating young people on the value of self-compassion, supporting them to believe in themselves.

Nick is a wonderful example of people who have managed to find a gift within their adversity. He often says that he does not have arms and hands to hold people but he doesn't need limbs because he can hold people with his heart.

The fourth pillar: Connect with your higher life purpose

Most people in society go through life on automatic pilot, like robots, simply doing the same thing day in and out. Many seem to be chasing after a dream of money, fame and material success, never taking the time to connect to their life purpose.

Connecting with your life purpose means that you dare to ask the big question. This big question is something that humans have been reflecting on since time immemorial. Each culture has within it some kind of reflective discipline, such as meditation, for example, to help us get in touch with the curiosity of why we are here in the first place and what is our purpose on earth.

So what is this big question? Different traditions and cultures look at this idea of the big question differently; here are some examples of this big question.

- If I am not my thought, feelings or sensations, then who or what am I?
- Who am I, why am I here and where am I going?
- What is the reason for existing in the first place?

As humans we take on roles in society: we may be a father, a mother, a worker, a sibling brother or a depressed person. These are just our roles and what we do; these are not really who we are in terms of our greater human potential. In terms of human consciousness we are far greater than these roles: we are human beings and not human doings.

Some ways in which we can get in touch with this higher human potential are: art and healing, spirituality, science and consciousness studies, music, drama and psychotherapy and so on.

Getting in touch with this concept can be immensely supportive when going through life and its challenges because it provides a certain sense of stability in the ever-changing modern life.

According to the Royal College of Psychiatrists, overall, some 25 per cent of women and 12 per cent of men suffer major depressive disorder during their lifetime. But people with a spiritual connection are up to 40 per cent less likely to get depressed than those who don't have such an connection.

Don't feel like you have to know the answer to this question. The blessing lies not in knowing the answer to the big question but rather in the posing of the question.

Understanding That the Power Is in the Now

The idea with mindfulness is to come back to the present moment where you can rest and feel safe in your own experience. Mindfulness helps you to connect to the beauty in this very moment however it may be. By tuning into the moment we can find a deep resource that can nurture and sustain us in a way never imagined. Recovery is an up and down process so it is helpful to take baby steps, making sure that we do what we can based on our ability and comfort levels.

This chapter contains a lot of information, but please don't rush; just take a deep breath and allow for things to unfold in their own way and in their own time.

Chapter 10

Living Mindfully Every Day

- -

In This Chapter

▶ Discovering the joy of going against the grain

▶ Learning to notice the difference between a bad day and a bad life

▶ Exploring how the nine mindful attitudes can help you connect with happiness

- -

*A*mongst many things, living mindfully means to live more fully in the present moment, away from the often negative habitual responses which so often cloud our ability to enjoy life. Cultivating mindfulness in your daily life empowers you to respond skilfully to the demands that modern life often brings. Mindfulness is not only a form of therapy, but ultimately it is a way of living and being. It is a creative process that helps you be fully human.

Above all, you don't need to have any particular problems or issues in order to practise and benefit from mindfulness. Schools teach it to help kids be calmer and help them learn and discover their own uniqueness. Artists use it to support the creative process, and the corporate sector uses it to help enhance emotional intelligence and resilience. Anyone can benefit from living more fully in the present moment whether he or she has a health condition or not.

Many people get into mindfulness because they simply want to enhance their sense of happiness. They may want to deepen their connection to themselves, their emotions and to life itself. In order to fully benefit from mindfulness it is helpful to begin to connect its practice with the rest of your life. There comes a moment in your practice where this art begins to merge with the rest of your life so that your whole life becomes an expression of this way of being.

In this chapter, I explore the nine mindful attitudes. I invite you to explore these for yourself in a way that works best for you.

The Joy of Going against the Grain

As people we often invest a lot of our energy in making sure that our life is materially successful, and yes, it is true that we need to have enough money to make sure that our needs are fully met. However, studies suggest that there is no direct correlation between wealth and happiness. In fact, research shows that some of the richest countries have the highest rates of depression. This lends weight to the proverb 'money can't buy happiness'.

What this all suggests is that if you want a life of true happiness you need to invest your time and effort in developing yourself as a person rather than only investing in material possessions.

In order to do this you have to step back from the current norm of how everyone in society thinks and behaves and begin to develop core attitudes that will help you support true happiness.

In many ways, you need to rediscover the antidotes to that which makes you unhappy and focus on developing the attitudes and core values that will help you cultivate a greater sense of wellbeing, joy and happiness. In this chapter, we explore the nine mindful attitudes or the protectors of happiness.

When money doesn't cut it . . .

Research conducted at Columbia University found that adolescents reared in suburban homes with an average family income of $120,000 report higher rates of depression, anxiety and substance abuse than any other socioeconomic group of young Americans today.

Going against the grain means that we invest our energy in attitudes that ultimately help us feel truly happy. It does not mean cutting yourself off from other people. On the contrary, it means that you begin to connect with people who are on a similar wavelength mentally. Doing so can be an immensely fulfilling and enjoyable experience.

Nine Mindful Attitudes: The Protectors of Happiness

Mindfulness involves nine mental attitudes which can help you live in a mindful and joyful way. These were reintroduced into modern secular mindfulness by Dr Jon Kabat-Zinn, PhD, a Professor of Medicine Emeritus and creator of the Mindfulness Based Stress Reduction (MBSR) programme at the University of Massachusetts Medical School. These attitudes are universal and do not belong to any particular tradition or school of thought; they are inherently present in most cultures and forms of philosophy as well as spirituality.

You can look at these attitudes as elements of mindfulness practice itself. Some argue that you cannot have mindfulness without these attitudes. The nine attitudes are antidotes to depression and protectors of happiness and emotional stability. This means that the more you apply these core attitudes, and live your life in attunement and alignment with them, the calmer, more emotionally stable and happier you will be.

One way to practise these attitudes is to simply choose one for the day, give yourself time to reflect on it and see if you can begin to apply it any of the major areas of your life, such as work, relationships, eating or parenting. There are no quick tips or ways of developing these. You can, however, invite yourself to reflect on these and explore possible ways of applying them to your day-to-day life.

The more willing you can begin to explore and begin to integrate these mindful attitudes into your life the more likely it is that you will begin to transform your life for the better.

Beginner's mind

Beginner's mind is a mental quality which encourages the idea that it is okay not to know something. Often we can feel like we have to be the expert, knowing or wanting to know everything, so we naturally feel very uncomfortable when we don't know something.

Beginner's mind is more like seeing yourself as a student of life. The lessons that life offers you never end, so you never stop being a student. The more open and willing you are to learning about yourself the more enjoyable, interesting and rewarding life will be.

If you firmly believe and are convinced that you know all there is to know about your condition, and how regain your sense of happiness, and are not open to any new ideas then you will not be able to learn, improve or progress.

Acceptance

Acceptance of the way things are right now, even if they are not pleasant or the way you want them to be, is the door to healing and recovery. Often one can misunderstand the idea of acceptance as a kind of giving up and resigning oneself to the difficulty of depression. Acceptance is not giving up; in fact it is quite the opposite. Cultivating the quality of acceptance is a very dynamic and active process of working with your difficulties. There are many stages to acceptance and it often takes time.

You can begin this process by simply putting out the welcome mat for whatever aspect of depression you are struggling with. By doing this you can begin to recognise that there is a difficulty, and begin to find the skills needed to bring about a positive change. Above all, remember that 'Rome wasn't built in one day' and that healing is a journey.

Patience

Often we try to hurry things up. Most people feel like this, including those who are not suffering from depression. We can often be impatient with ourselves as well as with others. Unfortunately, this only leads to further frustration and unhappiness.

Patience reminds us that there is often a process taking place, a journey – in other words, our life is unfolding. Trying to force yourself to feel happier or trying to make your recovery go faster in most cases does not really work. Patience teaches you that everything has its own rhythm and process. Life is a process and often things take time to change for the better. Unfortunately we can't always see the unfoldment and positive change, either because it is not noticeable enough or because we are unwilling to notice the positive changes in our own life.

Cultivating patience is a healing and restorative activity, and helps you to be able to hang in there and trust that if you stay committed to supporting yourself, your life will eventually improve.

Trust

Part of your journey to regaining happiness means that you begin to trust your own mind. When you feel down and ill you can often feel that your mind is your worst enemy. You can feel like you are unable to fully take care of yourself. This is totally understandable and okay. Cultivating trust is based on the fundamental reality that you are already in many ways trusting yourself. For example, you can trust that your body will take care of you. You don't have to worry or make sure that the heart beats. You just trust that it will continue to do so. In a similar way, you can slowly begin to trust your own ability to take care of yourself and be in a better position to manage your mood and wellbeing.

With time and regular mindfulness practice you will regain your trust in your mind and develop the sense that your mind is your own best friend; this can take time, but it is totally possible.

Non-judging

Judging is a normal quality of mind. We all have it and we all do it.

It's the 'I want this but don't want that' quality of mind. It's the constant preference and choosing that goes on all the time. Judging in many ways also means that you are not being okay with yourself and feeling that you are bad in some way for feeling or being a certain way. If you want to feel happy you would benefit from cultivating non-judgement, which means that you give permission for your feelings to be just as they are without telling yourself that you are bad in some way.

Practising non-judgement also means that you are a little bit kinder to yourself and try not to judge the judging itself and allow yourself to make mistakes and learn to be okay with them.

You may feel like you wanted to go outside for a walk then all of a sudden your mood dropped and you lost the motivation. Feeling disappointed in yourself, you then start beating yourself up for it. Being non-judgemental means that you would try to be okay about your mood change and disappointment, allowing yourself to have more kindness and say 'it is okay for me to feel this way, I could try again tomorrow'.

Non-striving

Non-striving is a lot about living your life in the present moment away from constant mental to-do lists. I don't know about you, but I often feel like I need to be somewhere other than where I am now, as if this moment is not good enough. I also often feel that I have to achieve something in order to feel good about myself. Non-striving teaches you to be more comfortable with the way things are right now and prevents you from getting too caught up in harsh expectation you might have of yourself. You can apply this attitude to your own recovery and remind yourself that your situation will change when the time is ready for it to change. Having a non-striving attitude towards your own recovery reminds you that recovery is a process which takes time and it allows for things to unfold in a way that is right for you.

Living in the present moment away from unrealistic future-orientated goals helps you to reduce depression as well as enhance your sense of joy and happiness.

Letting go

Letting go is the doorway to true happiness. It is human nature to cling to past experiences: to hurts, feelings and events which are long gone. The more you hold on to these the more you get caught up in them, which only makes you feel worse.

Everyone struggles with the idea of letting go, and people often think that it's something they *must* do, as if it's something that can be forced. You can't force letting go but you can practise and allow it.

True letting go is based on the idea that it is something you can do and are already doing; you do it without even realising. Each time you take a breath you have to let it go in order to make space for the new breath. You let go of the breath automatically, which means that you already know how to do it. The more you practise mindfulness the more easily you will be able to let go and drop certain unhelpful and negative emotions, thoughts and attitudes.

Rather than forcing yourself to let go of a certain feelings, simply remind yourself that letting go happens more readily and easily when you practise mindfulness. This means that the more you practise the more you can naturally let go and live in the moment.

Gratitude

In life people often take many things for granted. People often focus on what they don't have, thinking that if only they had this or that then they would truly be happy. Focusing on lack of the good in your life only breeds more lack and scarcity. Cultivating the attitude of generosity means that we acknowledge the good things which we already have. Our health – even if you are ill there are parts of you that are healthy – your friends or people who support you, the fact that you have a place to live, the fact that you have food to eat and so on. It is interesting that people are usually reminded of how fortunate they are only when they lose what they took for granted. For example, if your car breaks down and you can't drive to work, you suddenly miss that car, no matter how much you may have taken it for granted. All of a sudden the frustration of this situation can remind you how fortunate you were to have a car in the first place.

By practising gratitude you allow for more happiness to enter your life. We cannot really be happy if we do not recognise the good which is already here.

You may want to start a gratitude diary and write down each day one thing that you are thankful for. After doing it for a week or so, read through all the entries to remind yourself of all the things that you are grateful for.

Generosity

There are many different ways in which you could practise generosity. One way to receive happiness is to share your time and energy with others. When you give your attention to others it not only takes the focus off your own negative preoccupation but it actually benefits the other person as well. It is this shift of self-focus to focusing on others that is incredibly restorative and can help healing. You can give so many things which don't cost anything, such as your attention, your time, your smile and so on.

Being generous does not mean that you do not look after your own needs and try to save others. Rather it means that you share of yourself in a way that is comfortable to you.

You have friends over for lunch and you do the cooking. You can do so freely and happily because you enjoy it and know that they will also enjoy your food and be thankful for the effort that you made. This is one way to practise generosity, simply by cooking for others.

Happiness Embraces Unhappiness

If you have ever been in a happy personal relationship with someone you will know how satisfying and wonderful it is. You feel connected and valued and you know that you have someone who not only cares for you but also wants what is best for you. Having said that, you know that it's not always so blissful; being in a relationship can be hard work and often friction, discomfort and unhappiness arise as a result of the interaction between you and your partner.

Well, life in general is the same. There are many moments in life which are satisfying and beautiful but also there are times when life is a struggle. But I guess I am not telling you anything new, right? Often people get a wrong view, believing that life should be happy all the time and it's almost as if any kind of sadness is seen as bad. This kind of attitude can often lead to a shallow and partial experience of the way life really is.

As you practise mindfulness and continue to heal and grow you will be able to differentiate between noticing the 'unhappiness and struggle' that is a normal part of life from the 'chronic unhappiness' that is part of the experience of having depression. Sadness and bad days are a normal part of life whereas depression is a mental health condition that is characterized by a continuous low mood and sadness.

If you deny the existence of unhappiness and only wish for bliss, then not only will this lead to further unhappiness, but in many ways you will not really be allowing yourself to be fully alive.

Mindfulness helps you understand the reality that in order to feel truly happy you need to find a way of making peace with all of life. It is in the acceptance of this that you make a shift to living life more fully – not by denying the pain but by beginning to find a creative way to work with it, using greater skill and self-compassion.

It's a Bad Day, Not a Bad Life

Pretty much all people have bad days where they feel low, frustrated and down in some way. This is the nature of life. Some days are happy, some are not. Being able to accept this and having a way of navigating through this is what will help you stay centred and balanced in your day-to-day life.

When you feel depressed it can be very difficult to see things in this way, and very often life seems to be filled with so many bad days that they simply take over and make you feel like you have a bad life.

Reminding yourself that there might be a valid reason why you feel down on some days can be helpful. The fact is not all low mood is due to your illness. There can be actual reasons why you might be feeling more anxious or low on some days than on others.

We can often encounter situations in life which are difficult by their very nature.

For example, you partner might come back from work feeling irritable, and it seems like he or she doesn't want to talk to you. You might feel that this is your fault and in some way you have caused it, but the truth is very far from this. It can be that your partner had a hard day at work and simply, for whatever reason, does not feel able to communicate this to you.

Now, this situation where you feel something is not right and you feel that your partner is not communicating would make anyone feel anxious, frustrated, and sad in some way. Reacting in this way is a healthy human response to difficult situations.

Just because you are feeling down as a result of this situation does not mean that this is necessarily because of your condition. Having this reaction is very healthy and part of being a human being.

In many ways when you are depressed you can potentially feel like your reactions are not valid and that it's your illness making you feel this way. It's almost as if your whole life is bad and overcome with low mood, anxiety and feelings of extreme unhappiness, and it's hard to see the difference between a healthy emotional reaction and the type of intense negative thinking and rumination experienced in depression.

The fact is some emotional reactions are still valid even if they are not happy and pleasant. Beginning to see the validity of your reactions is a sign that you are beginning to get better.

Developing the skill where you encourage yourself to notice the difference between the valid and healthy emotional reactions and the habitual negative depressive reactions which are common to people suffering with depression will help you tremendously on your journey to healing through your condition.

As you begin to practise mindfulness and slowly recover, you will notice that you will develop greater skill in managing your thoughts, feelings and mood and you will begin to discover times in your day when your mood is better and you feel more relaxed and happy. As you begin to experience this, the massive heavy cloud of depression will begin to lift and you will once again be able to see some of the clear horizon.

Begin to notice when and where you feel less depressed and a little bit more relaxed. In other words, begin taking stock and check whether there is any difference in your mood in the course of the day. Noticing these changes in mood can help you connect with the possibility of managing your mood more effectively and so making it possible for you to regain your happiness.

Chapter 11

Taking the Next Step

I sincerely hope that reading this book will in some way inspire you to continue exploring mindfulness. It is possible that a question of what to do next will arise in your mind. In other words, 'What do I do now, and how can I continue to apply this knowledge to my life?' Recovering from depression is a life journey filled with many ups and downs. Having mindfulness as a technique in your toolkit not only empowers you to manage your condition more creatively and effectively, but more importantly it enables you to live life more joyfully. With regular mindfulness practice it is possible that you can learn to live well despite your illness and begin to rebuild a happy and meaningful life.

This continued journey through mindfulness can take many different forms and shapes. For some people, reading more books makes sense, as they feel they are not yet entirely sure whether mindfulness is actually for them. For other people, it means simply taking the time to reflect on some of the ideas presented in this book. Others continue their process of exploration by joining a mindfulness based course whilst others feel ready to have one-to-one mindfulness sessions. Perhaps you simply want to start listening to a mindfulness CD and support your own emotional and mental wellbeing that way. There is no right or wrong way. There simply is just your way. The important thing is not to rush things in any way but rather take the time to ask yourself what it is that you want to do and what it is that you are ready for right now.

In this chapter, I help you explore some possible ways in which you can take the next step in a way that feels right for you.

Remembering You Don't Need to Do It Alone

Reaching out for support is a sign of taking the next step. When you are depressed reaching out for help can be extremely difficult. This is partly because of the stigma around depression. People who are affected by the condition can feel fearful of being rejected or in some way thought of being as a less of a person.

Research suggests that people who ask for help when faced with illness have a higher chance of recovering than those who stay isolated. In many ways, it is important to accept that you actually cannot do it alone and need the support of others. Healing through depression needs the inclusion of other people who have your needs at their heart. Coming to this point of acceptance can sometimes take a long time, and this is okay too. In time you will find it within yourself to be brave enough to reach out for help. Yes, it does take courage, but you can reach out in a way that is safe and reasonably comfortable.

 It is okay to feel scared, but at the same time your chances of getting better are greater when you ask for guidance and support. Reaching out for help can mean different things to different people. Some people prefer to share their problem with their family whilst others prefer to speak to their doctor or counsellor. Above all, find your own way of reaching out in a way that works for you.

Considering a Mindfulness Course

Another way of taking the next step is to consider joining a mindfulness course. Participating in a course can be a very rewarding and empowering experience. There is something extremely nourishing about learning mindfulness as part of a group. You get to experience the community connection and will have an opportunity to learn from other people's experiences as well as share your own reflections with the group. There are many types of mindfulness-based courses but they are mostly of two types:

- ✔ Mindfulness Based Stress Reduction (MBSR)
- ✔ Mindfulness Based Cognitive Therapy (MBCT)

Both MBSR and MBCT are pretty much the same in structure and are generally eight weeks long, meeting once a week for two and a half hours. The main difference being that MBSR is more generic and focuses on helping people suffering with stress or illness, as well as supporting people who simply want to learn mindfulness in order to enhance their creativity, performance or emotional intelligence. MBCT, on the other hand, focuses on helping people who have had three or more episodes of depression and are currently well. In other words, the goal of the MBCT course is to help you stay well so that you do not get depressed again.

It is useful to remember that a mindfulness course is not a form of group therapy, and you don't have to share or talk about your own troubles. This fact can be quite reassuring for some people. Also, doing the course takes commitment, and you need to feel ready for it. It is not a good idea to participate in a course if you are in the midst of a crisis or when your mood is so low that it prevents you from going about your day.

 Prior to joining a course, make sure that you speak to the course organiser. Ask all the questions that you feel you need answered. The course organiser will help you explore whether participating in the course is right for you.

Taking a Mindful Approach to Antidepressant Medication

Many people turn to medication in order to help them cope with the effects of depression. Taking antidepressant medication has some good benefits, but doing so also has some drawbacks. Nowadays resources are tight and doctors only have a short amount of time in which to take care to listen to their patients. It is no surprise that antidepressant medication is the first thing that most doctors would offer you should you ever visit their consulting room asking for help.

I too have taken medication to help me cope with depression and have found it helpful. Many people do not want to take antidepressants due to side effects or due to personal reasons. It is helpful to know that there are other alternatives, and that there is a choice. In this section, I shed some light around the topic of modern antidepressants and also offer some possible alternatives.

Whether to take meditation or not is a personal choice, and you should never feel coerced or forced by anyone into taking medication if you feel strongly against it. Be flexible and, if offered medication, ask for all the details about the drug before making up your mind. Take your time so that you can make a well-informed decision.

Types of antidepressant drugs

Following are the five major types of medication that a medical doctor might prescribe for your depression:

- ✔ **Selective Serotonin Reuptake Inhibitor (SSRI):** This group of drugs, which includes Prozac and Cipramil, is most commonly prescribed for depression as these types of drugs have fewer side effects compared to some of the older versions.

- ✔ **Serotonin-Noradrenaline Reuptake Inhibitor (SNRI):** This category, which includes Cymbalta and Efexor, is also fairly new and is similar to the SSRI category. Some people seem to respond better to SSRIs while others respond better to SNRIs.

- ✔ **Tricyclic Antidepressant (TCA):** This group, which includes Elavil (amitriptyline), is an older one. Drugs of this type are no longer usually recommended as a first-line treatment for depression mainly because they can be more dangerous if an overdose is taken and because their side-effects can be more unpleasant.

- ✔ **Monoamine oxidase inhibitor (MAOI):** This category, which includes Parnate and Nardil, is another older one. Some of the side-effects can be very serious, so they are only used under the strict supervision of a psychiatrist.

> ✔ **Benzodiazepine:** Valium and Xanax are part of this group. Although these drugs are not antidepressants themselves, they can often be prescribed in conjunction with antidepressant medication, especially when there is severe anxiety or when sleep is affected as well. These types of drugs are extremely addictive and should only be used for a short period of time.

Considering medication effectiveness

Whether antidepressants are actually useful is debatable. There is some research that suggests that sugar pills or the use of placebo is just as effective in treating mild to moderate depression as are modern antidepressants. Other research suggests just under a quarter of patients do not respond well to drug treatment and in fact do worse on antidepressants than patients who were given a placebo or sugar pills.

According to The Royal College of Psychiatrists 50% to 65% of people treated with an antidepressant for depression will see an improvement, compared to 25% to 30% of those taking inactive 'sugar' pills (placebo). What this suggests is that most people do benefit from antidepressants, even if it is sometimes a result of the placebo effect.

Whatever the research says, the important thing is to be well informed so that you can make a better and more informed decision as to whether antidepressants are a good choice for you.

Weighing the pros and cons of medication

Antidepressants can be very helpful in treating depression, but they can have some serious side-effects. Long term they can potentially cause damage to your body. This does not mean that I am encouraging you not to take medication, nor am I saying that you should come off your antidepressants if you are already on them. My intention here is to simply inform you so that you can make the best decision for you. Let us now look at some of the pros and cons when it comes to antidepressant drugs.

Following are some advantages of antidepressants:

✔ **Getting some space from painful emotions.** When we feel overwhelmed by painful feelings it can make it very difficult to function. Antidepressants in many ways numb these intense feelings so that you can better cope with your own emotions.

✔ **Helps you to function.** Low mood, physical pain and discomfort are some of the symptoms of depression. Medication can help improve your mood as well as help alleviate some of the symptoms of depression such as fatigue, physical discomfort and pain as well as poor sleep.

✔ **Cheaper and easier alternative.** Antidepressants are much cheaper and easier to take than other forms of talking therapies where you need to be able to show commitment to attending therapy sessions. This is the main reason why doctors prescribe them as a first choice of treatment. It is also true that not everyone wants to have therapy or is at the right place in his or her life to receive it.

Following are some possible disadvantages of antidepressants:

✔ **Dangerous side-effects.** Some antidepressants can have severe and debilitating side-effects such as weight gain and changes in personality, to name just two. Some people have reported feeling suicidal when on antidepressants. In some cases, these people had no history of suicidal thoughts prior to taking the drugs.

✔ **Finding a suitable medication takes time.** Some types of medication work for people; others don't. Often, it can take time to figure out which drug works best for a particular person. Some people go through two to four types of medication before they find the one that is of some benefit to them. Also, it can take anywhere from three to five weeks before you feel any benefits whatsoever. This process can be very debilitating due to the experience of side-effects.

✔ **Can negatively affect emotional recovery.** Prolonged use of antidepressants changes your brain chemistry. It can change the way you think and feel and process information. It is possible that this can negatively affect your ability to process and experience emotions such as grief and other painful feelings, which is necessary in order for you to come to terms and heal psychologically. Some people who take antidepressants report that they lose their ability to feel any sadness or happiness, ending up feeling nothing at all.

✔ **Difficult to come off drugs.** Many people report that once they have started using antidepressants they find it very hard to come off them. Antidepressants are thought not to be physically addictive, but stopping them abruptly can cause adverse changes in your brain chemistry, which can make you feel very unwell. It is best to stop slowly in phases and only under the supervision of a qualified health professional.

Above all, information is power and the more informed you are the more you will be able to choose that which you feel is right for you.

Also keep in mind that what is right for you changes! It might be that at this time in your journey taking medication is right, or it might be that you feel that at this very moment you might not need medication but might do so later in your journey. Stay flexible and listen to your own needs.

My personal experience with medication

For me personally, the biggest benefit for taking antidepressants was that I felt that the numbness caused by the medication protected me from the intense feelings I was simply not ready to feel or face.

It was like the drugs caused a comfortable protective wall between me and my emotions, and I was very thankful for this wall. I simply wasn't ready to feel all the mess that was inside me. As time went on, I felt ready to get more in touch with the depth of my own emotional reality. I began feeling the disadvantages of feeling numb and medicated and felt that I wanted to break free from what felt like being in a chemical straightjacket.

It was scary and it took a long time before I could finally stop the medication. I had to get used to my internal landscape of thoughts, feelings and emotions. In many ways, I had to learn how to feel again. Mindfulness has empowered me to work with this experience more effectively as well as more creatively. The more willing I was to look at my own suppressed emotions, the more I developed an ability to feel safe with my feelings, being more comfortable in my own skin so to speak. It took time, lots of support, commitment, patience and trust in the process of healing itself.

When to consider coming off

Taking antidepressants could be a good way of taking the next step. Deciding to stay on medication can also be considered as taking the next step. But what if you are thinking about coming off medication? Is this a good or bad idea? Thinking about coming off antidepressants could also be considered as taking the next step, but it can also be considered as taking a step back.

I do not want to make generalisations, but if you are reading this book you are probably on medication already. Your question might be around coming off medication rather than whether to take them or not.

I am not here to tell you whether you should start taking, stay on or come off your antidepressants. Only you can decide this for yourself. It is important to also include your chosen healthcare professional in this decision, and it is not a good idea to come off your meditation without his or her support.

What I do want to say is that with regular mindfulness practice, patience and commitment it is definitely possible to come off medication if that is something that you decide is right for you. Knowing this in itself can be helpful, and to know that many others have done so is empowering.

So you might say, 'Okay, I want to stop medication. When is a good time to do it?' Again, only you can decide that; however, here are a few pointers for you to consider:

✔ **Only you will know when the time is right for you to come off medication.** You will know intuitively. If you are not sure, you are not ready. It's as simple as that. In either case if you are unsure then please consult your chosen healthcare professional for support and advice.

✔ **Don't try to stop your medication just because you don't like being on drugs.** It's okay to take antidepressants. Some people feel like they are less of a person because they are on medication. Use whatever works for you and helps you take care of yourself.

✔ **The more you invest in yourself by practising mindfulness, getting the right support (such as counselling),**

eating well and exercising more, the less likely you will
need continued medication.

✔ **Talk to your chosen healthcare professional and get
his or her support.** Do not stop your medication on your
own, as complications can arise.

If your health professional disagrees and chooses not
to support you then make sure you understand his or
her reasons. If you still feel strongly about stopping then
consider finding another professional to get a second
opinion.

✔ **Consider exploring natural alternatives.** There are many
natural antidepressants that you can use instead of the
modern drugs. Never self-medicate, however. Always consult a health professional qualified in the relevant field.

When you come off medication you will have to begin to find
the courage and be willing to face all the feelings that the
antidepressants have helped you to keep at bay by numbing.

Potentially there really does come a point in your recovery
when you might feel ready to befriend these emotions. These
feelings don't just disappear, and it's a wonderful thing when
they do start to surface. This resurfacing of emotions can be
very uncomfortable at first, but it means that you are beginning to once again feel more fully. This is what being a human
being means, to feel all that we can, but feel it in a way that
helps us evolve and grow rather than contract and lose our
emotional balance.

Trying Out Natural
Healing Methods

Natural healing focuses on supporting the whole person and
looks at supporting the body and mind so that both may
return to a natural state of balance. Natural healing methods
such as nutrition, movement and herbal medicine are just
some of the healing methods that can dramatically contribute to your recovery and help enhance your sense of mental,
physical and emotional wellbeing.

If for whatever reason you decide that modern antidepressants are not for you then you may find it of benefit to explore natural healing. In this section, I cover just a few options available: herbal medicine, nutrition and mindful movement. These natural alternatives can provide you with safe and effective ways of helping you manage your condition more effectively and naturally.

When consulting a natural health practitioner, make sure that he or she is qualified and registered in his or her respective profession. It might also be a good idea to call this person and ask about his or her experience in treating individuals with depression.

Supporting your mood with herbal medicine

Herbal medicine is the oldest form of medicine known. Many of the modern drugs in medicine today originate from the ancient herbal healing systems. There are many types of herbal medicine systems. Some originate in Europe, China, and India as well as many other countries.

In the UK, medical herbalists are healthcare providers trained in Western orthodox medical diagnosis who use medicines made from plants to treat their patients. In the UK, medical herbalists have the right to diagnose illness. The National Institute of Medical Herbalists was founded in 1864 in the UK and is one of the oldest Western institutions that provides training and registration for medical herbalists.

One of the most famous and effective herbal remedies that has been researched extensively for depression is *St John's Wort* (or *Hypericum Perforatum* in Latin). Some researchers suggest that St John's Wort is just as effective as the modern antidepressant drug Prozac, but without the side-effects. Whether this is true is another question, but research into the effectiveness of this remedy is very promising. What is conclusive is that St John's Wort is extremely effective in treating mild to moderate depression as well as anxiety with almost no side-effects.

There are two main chemical compounds in St John's Wort that help regulate and enhance mood in people suffering from depression. These natural compounds are called *hypericin* and *hyperforin* and act on chemical messengers in the nervous system that regulate mood.

Do not self-medicate! Always consult your medical doctor or medical herbalist before taking any herbal medicines, especially if you are taking other antidepressants.

Nutrition for the brain

Another way to take the next step is to revisit how and what you eat. Modern life, with its fast pace and fast food, does little to nourish or sooth our minds. In fact, our brains are literally depleted of vital nutrients, affecting our mood and levels of wellbeing. Underlying conditions, such as food sensitivities, blood sugar or hormone irregularities, could also be affecting your brain health.

The connection between the gut and brain also has a tremendous impact on mental health. Ninety per cent of serotonin (the naturally occurring chemical partly responsible for good mood) is produced in the gastrointestinal track. This suggests that there is a relationship between what we eat, the health of our gut and our mood.

Many studies show that foods high in sugar, poor unhealthy fats and refined carbs enhance the likelihood of depression. Removing the worst offenders for 'brain drain' such as sugar and processed food will have a positive effect reducing inflammation and immune over-reactions, which can manifest as mood swings and memory loss. Learning to balance blood sugar will also provide a more steady supply of energy to the brain which will help stabilise your mood levels.

Amino acids from protein are needed to create important brain chemical messengers called *neurotransmitters*. For example, turkey, eggs and seafood are high in tryptophan, which creates serotonin.

Fats make up most of our brain and help us to feel satisfied, preventing cravings. Choosing high quality healthy fats will ensure the smooth running of the brain and can help relieve depressive symptoms. These healthy fats can be found in foods such as oily fish, butter, coconut oil, avocados, nuts and seeds.

Another good way of helping your brain is to keep it hydrated by drinking lots of good-quality filtered or mineral water. Some research suggests that we just don't drink enough water, which can contribute to poor cognitive function as well as low mood.

One way of exploring how nutrition can help manage your mood is to visit a qualified nutritional practitioner who specialises in treating people with depression.

Mindful movement with yoga, chi kung and tai chi

Movement and exercise have been used for thousands of years to help people with many different health conditions, including depression.

Mindful movement exercises are easy, low impact, slow movements that combine specifically designed postures, meditation and a special way of breathing. Usually the breathing is done very slowly and mindfully, which enhances oxygen levels in the brain. It also helps to calm down the part of the brain called the *amygdala*, which is overactive when we are either experiencing stress or depression. Yoga and other mindful movement exercises also help to increase levels of *gamma-amino butyric acid* (GABA) in the brain, which leads to a calmer mind and better mood. (GABA is an amino acid which acts as a neurotransmitter in the central nervous system. It inhibits nerve transmission in the brain, calming nervous activity.)

Consider signing up for a yoga class or other form of mindful movement. Being amongst other people can also be very nourishing and help you feel better.

When Not to Use Mindfulness in Depression – Contraindications

Mindfulness is not a cure-all. It is important to know that there are depressive conditions where using mindfulness can potentially make your condition worse.

If you are suffering from severe or clinical depression it is best to seek professional advice before starting to use any of the techniques suggested in this book.

In my experience, you can still benefit from mindfulness practice even if you are severely depressed, but this needs to be offered under the special guidance of a health professional who has the experience not only in treating people with depression but also in utilising mindfulness. In this way you can begin to learn mindfulness in the company of a person who embodies the qualities of support, empathy, skill, mindfulness and compassion.

When to Seek Emergency Help – A Note on Suicidal Thoughts

Feeling extremely low in mood as well as experiencing a sense of utter hopelessness is often a symptom of depression. Some people who are affected with the condition also experience thoughts of wanting to end their life. Psychologists call this *suicidal ideation*.

Having thoughts of wanting to end your life is not uncommon in depression, but it is important to know that there is a difference between thinking about ending your life to actively planning it to actually going through with the plan and attempting suicide.

Most people can think about ending their life but never actually act on their ideas and go through with it.

Some people have a deep feeling of shame for having such thoughts and it can feel extremely difficult to even begin to consider talking to anyone about your thoughts and feelings when you are affected by suicidal thoughts.

It is possible you might probably want to withdraw and isolate yourself. Please remember that this will only make things worse. If thoughts about ending your life are constantly on your mind, seek support immediately as they are not going to get better on their own.

Consider telling your trusted friend, your doctor or minister or whomever you feel comfortable talking to.

If you feel that you might hurt yourself or are contemplating going through with your plans to end your life, seek emergency help at once. Do not delay! Contact your ambulance service or visit your nearest Accident and Emergency hospital department where they will be more than happy to assist you and support you.

Part IV
The Part of Tens

Discover ten tips for finding the motivation to get better in a free article at www.dummies.com/extras/managingdepressionwithmindfulness.

In this part . . .

✔ Take a look at ten ways to prevent relapse and stay well.

✔ Find out how to get the most out of mindfulness.

Chapter 12

Ten Tips for Preventing Relapse and Staying Well

● ●

In This Chapter

▶ Having a daily routine to help you stay well

▶ Taking time out to nurture and take care of yourself

▶ Becoming aware of your triggers and learning to manage them more skilfully

● ●

*M*y wish for you is, of course, that you stay well and do not relapse. However, I know from experience that relapsing into depression is part of the journey of living well with the condition. Sometimes you can't avoid relapsing, and if for some reason you do, the relapse need not be completely devastating if you know that you have the tools to pull yourself out again. This chapter covers some of the most helpful tools for staying well.

Take Time to Care for Yourself

One incredibly helpful thing to do is to begin to be more comfortable with taking time out for yourself. Often we feel guilty for doing this and thoughts like 'I am selfish for taking time for myself' can creep in. This is normal for everyone who starts on the journey to practising mindfulness, and is not unique to people suffering from depression.

One way of challenging the idea that you're selfish is to think that when you take time to take care of yourself, you also enhance your capacity to be open and happy with others. So in a way you are not only investing in yourself but also in your relationships with your friends and family, who will be so much happier when you are happier. If you struggle to take time out for your, then that's okay: just welcome the struggle, be curious about it and shift your attention to the benefits of taking care of yourself.

Schedule in a time once a day when you can be just with yourself, undisturbed by telephones, emails and other distractions. You may want to do a mindfulness practice, go for a walk, take a bath, read a good book, call a friend or do whatever you enjoy that gives you a feeling of being taken care of.

Develop a Regular Mindfulness Practice

Having a daily regular practice can be of great support in managing our mood and enhancing our sense of wellbeing.

A couple of ways of practising mindfulness exist. They are:

- ✔ Constantly reflect and think about mindful ideas and attitudes; doing this will help you reframe or change some of the negative beliefs that contribute to your depression.
- ✔ Actually do any of the short mindfulness exercises. This can be a 3-minute breathing space or any of the longer 15- or 20-minute mindfulness exercises.

Personally, I struggled with the exercise practice part for a long time and simply continued to reflect over and over on the positive and helpful mindful attitudes, such as patience and self-compassion. After some time these helpful ideas began sinking into my mind and I developed the courage to begin to practise the actual mindfulness exercises.

In actual fact, the two methods, the reflection on mindful attitudes and the practical exercises, are part of the totality of the practice of mindfulness, like the two wings of a bird synchronised in full flowing harmony.

In my personal and clinical experience, people with depression have a very low capacity to sit and be silent with themselves, so doing the mindfulness exercises can be challenging at first.

It is, however, definitely possible if you begin with very short five-minute exercises.

Begin with a very easy and effective exercise called the five-minute breathing space. It only lasts five minutes. The practice is included in Chapter 7.

Do this every day at a set time of the day and simply notice what the effect is: don't judge the experience, just notice what it is. The benefits of having a daily practice are numerous and a little mindfulness practice is better than none.

Have a Crisis Plan: Hope for the Best, Prepare for the Worst

There is an approach within mental health recovery called the *Wellness Recovery Action Plan* (WRAP). This is a plan that you can put together with the support of a trusted person, such as a friend or your counsellor. This plan is for your benefit, just in case you start feeling your depression getting worse. The WRAP can be very useful in situations when you feel that your ability to think positively and logically is in some way hindered, and can be of immense support to you in preventing your depression from getting worse.

The purpose of the crisis/WRAP plan is mainly to:

- ✓ Decrease and prevent intrusive or troubling feelings and behaviours
- ✓ Increase personal empowerment
- ✓ Improve quality of life
- ✓ Assist you in achieving your own life goals and dreams

Some of the points that can be included in the WRAP are:

- ✓ When I feel my mood is low for more than two days I will contact the following person for support.
- ✓ When I feel I need support I will contact the following person.

> ✔ When I feel I cannot control my intense feelings I will take the following helpful action.

The crises plan/WRAP plan needs to be prepared when you feel reasonably well beforehand and kept in a place that is easily accessible to you when you need it.

Keep the plan personalised for your unique circumstances. For more information on how to design a Crises/WRAP plan visit the Mental Health Foundation at `www.mentalhealth.org.uk/help-information/mental-health-a-z/R/recovery`.

Consider Community Involvement

One aspect of having depression is social isolation – the feeling that you are suffering all by yourself. Connecting with others in similar situations can be of great benefit to you, and help you feel like you are not alone in your pain and suffering.

There are a number of support groups that you can find in your area. You can use the Internet to identify the ones that you feel you would be comfortable exploring.

If you feel that you are not ready to meet people, or that groups are not your thing, then you may want to consider social media. There are a number of wonderful and helpful Internet-based groups that you can become part of. Whatever you choose make sure that you feel comfortable and always remember that you can choose to leave the group at any time.

List Your Triggers and Possible Ways to Manage Them

At times it might feel that the dark cloud of depression simply comes over you uninvited and without warning. At other times it happens more slowly and there might be certain triggers or signs that you are beginning to get worse. We call these relapse triggers *signatures* in the world of psychology.

For example, you might find that after you had had a fight with your partner, the next day you were finding it difficult to get out of bed in the morning. That might escalate so that you start spending time at home isolated for days on end.

So the trigger was the fight with your partner and the relapse signature or sign was that you have now begun to isolate yourself excessively again. This is a warning signal that your depression is possibly getting worse and that you need to take urgent action.

 Depression can get triggered by different things for different people and what affects one person negatively does not affect another in the same way.

 Try to identify at least some of your triggers and write them down. Next, think of ways that you could manage this situation more effectively as opposed to being overpowered by your not-so-helpful coping strategy – isolating yourself, for example. You can make the list as long as you like, and as personal and detailed as you want. Ask for support from a trusted person if needed to help you with this.

Do Some Mindful Exercise

Mindful exercise is different from the normal type of physical exercise in that the purpose is not so much to get fit but to bring enjoyment and explore exercise as another form of practising mindfulness, namely in movement.

The main benefit of mindful exercise is that it decreases negative rumination by shifting attention from our head space to sensations in the body. This creates a little bit of space and freedom from our negative mental tendencies. In other words, the more we are in our bodies, the less we are in our heads, and this can be a very good thing when it comes to living with depression.

Some research that suggests that exercise can help reduce symptoms of depression, mainly because of the release of the naturally occurring 'happy chemicals' in the brain called *endorphins*.

Choose an exercise that you can do mindfully, such as walking, for example. The next time you walk down the street, decide to do so mindfully. Be aware of the sensations under your feet and start noticing the environment around you, including the smells and the colours. Use all your five senses to connect with the outside world.

Mindful exercise takes some practice, but can be very enjoyable and effective in reducing *negative rumination*, a term for excessive and obsessive negative thinking.

Be Mindful of Your Thoughts

In my personal experience of living well with depression, I know that I have to be consistently mindful of my thoughts, the quality of my self-talk as well as my mood levels. By the way, this does not only apply to people living with depression but to anyone who wants to maintain a happy and productive life.

When you start noticing that your thoughts are of a self-critical or negative quality, this can serve as an indication that you need to take some action to help prevent them from intensifying and getting worse.

The more familiar we become with our mental habits, thoughts and feelings, the more effectively can we begin to navigate through them in a way that decreases the negative and unhelpful mental habits and enhances the positive and helpful ones.

Mindfulness is not like taking a pill and then becoming well and cured. You need to practise this method of mindfulness daily. Mindfulness does not only help prevent relapse, but it also enhances creativity, emotional intelligence and the feeling of being in the flow with life.

Negative, unhelpful thoughts lead to painful and negative feelings. These in turn lead to low mood and a potential to make us spiral into depression. Bringing a compassionate awareness to our day-to-day thoughts can protect us from getting lost in them and becoming depressed.

We all experience negative thoughts, but for those of us with depression negative thinking can trigger negative feelings and low mood which then in turn can potentially develop into recurrent depression.

Keep a diary of pleasant and unpleasant events. This will help you become more aware of the relationship between your thoughts, feelings, mood and behaviour.

Support Yourself with Music and Creativity

Part of recovering from depression and regaining our sense of mental and emotional wellbeing is to connect with the things that we enjoy and give us a natural feeling of happiness. Doing something creative can connect us with deep inner resources that would otherwise not be available to us. Listening to your favourite music can deeply enhance your sense of wellbeing. You can also use music to match your mood and to help you express certain emotions or it can be used to regulate and enhance certain feelings. Music is also an effective tool for raising your mood levels when you may be feeling low. Music is very much part of the creative domain so exploring what creativity means to you might be useful and could help you minimise the chance of relapse.

Another creative exercise is *biodanza*, which is a type of free flow dance. Painting and writing poetry can also be of immense support to use and help you with emotional expression.

Know and Respect Your Limits

Those of us who are living with depression are usually sensitive individuals and have a lower capacity to tolerate stress and excessive pressure. We would greatly benefit from getting to know our limits, and need to be mindful not to take on too many responsibilities.

Gradually developing the skills of noticing when you are taking on too much will minimise your stress and therefore the potential to relapse into depression.

Following are some examples of situations that can often contribute to your mood getting worse:

- ✔ Long working hours
- ✔ Always being there for others
- ✔ Lack of support with financial matters
- ✔ Worrying about physical health and putting off seeing a doctor
- ✔ Feeling the pressure to socialise every Saturday night

Life, people and situations will always put some pressure and demands on us, but we can learn to politely resist and be able to say no to others.

Too much stress or pressure can also trigger depression so the more relaxed we are and the more our life is in balance the more we will be able to protect ourselves from relapsing into depression. Therefore, knowing and respecting your limits can be of immense help in maintaining your sense of wellbeing.

Planning Your Day and Having a Routine

Developing a good supportive structure and routine can serve as protection against relapsing into depression and help you stay well. A good and healthy routine can minimise those unhelpful mental habits from taking over your life. You can positively manage the habit of staying in bed or sleeping excessively during the day, for example, by deciding the day before how long you are going to stay in bed, when you are going to get up, and what exactly it is that you are going to be doing that day. Planning your day the night before is the best way to bring in some helpful structure to your day.

The night before, make a short list of all the things that you need to attend to the next day, things that might be important – such as going to the bank or paying bills. Organise them in order of priority, including the time for your meals and some time to do something that you enjoy.

Chapter 13

Ten Tips for Getting the Most Out of Mindfulness

In This Chapter

▶ Effectively managing your negative chattering mind

▶ Learning to use the breath as support for calming your mind

▶ Enjoying the benefits of taking time out for yourself through self-nurture

*T*he question of how to get the most out of mindfulness is more of a question of how to get the most out of life: this is what we are really exploring here. By 'get the most out of life' I mean achieving personal understanding, self-compassion, calmness and the ability to feel like you have a choice, and in this way manage your depression more effectively.

In order to begin to get the most out of life we need to begin the journey of making mindfulness part of our lives. In other words, we need to begin integrating mindfulness into our day-to-day activities so that we can experience the benefits of being able to live with greater ease.

So how can you get the most out of mindfulness and therefore the most out of your life?

I invite you to use the effective tips in this chapter as and when you need them, and trust that they will support you in your efforts to cultivate a sense of greater emotional wellbeing.

Once a Day Do an Activity Mindfully

The way to get the most out of mindfulness and therefore out of life is to begin connecting it more with our lives in a practical way. One way of doing this is to begin exploring which of our daily activities could be done more mindfully.

Bringing more mindfulness to our daily activities – such as showering, for example – will help us be less caught up in our emotions, unhelpful thoughts and depression. In this way, we will focus and rest our attention more in the present moment on the task at hand, rather than in our heads.

The more you are aware of what you are doing right now, where your body is, the more grounded and stable you will be. This feeling of being grounded can then lead to a greater sense of mental and emotional wellbeing.

Decide on an activity that would be easy to apply mindfulness to, such as taking a shower or brushing your teeth, or anything else that you feel you would like to try. What might be easy for one person might not be for another. Make a conscious decision to simply give it a go and notice what happens.

What might help is to ask yourself 'Where is my body now? What am I doing right now?' Bring your attention to your five physical senses. If you are choosing to try a mindful shower, feel and sense the water flowing over your body, sense the temperature of the water. Try noticing new things about the experience.

Think and Reflect on Mindfulness as Often as You Can

Reflecting on mindful ideas – such as self-compassion, for example – can be an effective way to keep the subject alive in our minds and help us deepen our understanding of it. This is another way in which we can support our efforts in managing depression more creatively.

What it boils down to is how we use our minds.

On the one hand, we can let the mind do its crazy thing and bombard us with constant chatter, so making us lose our ground, while on the other side we can consciously choose what we think, with intention.

At this moment you might feel like you just would not be able to choose your thoughts, and if this is the case, then that's fairly normal, as most people feel this way. Having said this, once you start practising mindfulness, you will discover that you do in fact have this capacity to have more choice in what thoughts you do and do not give more attention to.

What I am proposing here is that you in some way gently begin to challenge yourself and choose to think about mindful ideas that will be of benefit to you on your journey through depression.

 Decide which aspect of mindfulness you need most right now, the one that would be helpful for you to explore. Then simply get interested in it. Read about it, watch some online videos on it and keep it (the topic) alive in your mind. Try typing **mindfulness** into YouTube and see what you can find which might be helpful.

Do the Practice – A Little Practice Is Better Than None

When we can begin to reflect more often on mindfulness and what it means to us, we begin to use our greater capacity for choice.

In order to get the most out of mindfulness we actually have to begin to practise it – and I really do mean practise it. It is when we begin to do the actual mindfulness exercises that we can start to rewire our brains and relate more optimistically to ourselves.

There are a number of easy exercises that you can begin to explore for yourself. Chapter 7 outlines some of these.

Mindfulness practice is divided into two categories, namely: formal and informal practice.

- ✔ **Formal practice** consists of the daily sitting or lying mindfulness exercises that are done in a safe and protected space. This is almost like the laboratory of our mind and body where we not only cultivate our capacity to calm and ground our minds, but also develop our innate capacity for self-compassion. Formal practice is most effective when you do it regularly at a specifically set time in the morning, afternoon or evening.

- ✔ **Informal practice** is the application of the techniques such as breathing and or wiggling and sensing our feet, for example, wherever we are or whatever we might be doing.

  So, for example, we can be sitting on the bus or waiting in the queue in the bank and we might start feeling anxious and preoccupied with unhelpful thoughts. It is here that we can begin to apply what we have learned in our formal practice.

You don't have to try hard to succeed in this but simply and slowly begin to explore this for yourself and remember that all it takes is to take a deep breath and wiggle your toes.

A little practice is better than none.

Get Used to Nurturing Yourself

Getting used to investing creative time in cultivating a sense of emotional wellbeing can really help you in reducing depression and developing a sense of wellbeing.

Unfortunately we live in a society which does not support taking time out for ourselves. We are constantly pushed to chase after material things and are bombarded daily by messages through advertisements and news that only perpetuate our sense of anxiety and unhappiness.

The idea of nurturing ourselves can be challenging for anyone, including people who are not affected with depression, so getting comfortable with this concept and way of life might or might not take some time.

Self-nurture can mean different things to different people. In essence it is creating some protected space for ourselves where we invest in our sense of wellbeing. It means setting aside some space for you so that you can grow and begin to heal, a time where you can be supported in your efforts. The very fact that you are reading this book means that you are already nurturing yourself.

The idea is to utilise your time more beneficially and enjoyably so that you can begin to heal and get the most out of life.

Self-nurturing can be:

- ✔ Taking time to practise mindfulness
- ✔ Watching more films that lift your mood
- ✔ Reading about topics that support your process of healing
- ✔ Going for a walk
- ✔ Talking to a friend
- ✔ Joining a mindfulness course
- ✔ Going for a weekly massage

I invite you to take some time to explore what nurturing yourself might mean to you.

Remind Yourself That You Have a Choice – You Can Be Mindless or Mindful

Those of us who know what depression is like know that the idea of having choice can be a hard one to swallow. It took me a long time to understand and then to experience this sense of having a choice of what I think and do.

Having said this, we choose all the time. We choose what we eat, what TV programmes we watch, whom we talk to and so on. The capacity to choose how we think and behave is inherent within us. We have this ability by default, because we are human.

It can be a big revelation to understand that at any time we can take a deep breath, and that this will help us be more mindful. We don't have to believe that we can do it: we simply do it and the more we do it the more we develop a new habit, which will become a supportive way of managing our condition.

You may want to wear a coloured elastic band as an aid to help remind you that you can disengage from the mindless chatter and be more mindful. Each time you look at it you will be reminded to take a deep breath.

Go Slowly and Gently

Encouraging yourself to slow down your pace of life and go gently can dramatically help you to manage your mood more effectively.

This going gently is based on the understanding that healing through depression can take time, and realistically you can't really know how long it will take. With the right support, for some it can take weeks, for others months and yet for others years, before long we come to a point where we begin to live well with depression and our life rather than suffering from it.

Learning to manage our mood, mental patterns and emotions is a process of discovery with many ups and downs. Some days your mood feels better and other days feels low. With regular mindfulness practice and support, things will improve, as will your ability to manage your life more effectively.

Reminding yourself of the following points might help you to go gently:

- ✔ Understand that this journey will take as long as it needs to take.

✔ See your recovery as a journey rather than simply trying to fix something that you think might be wrong with you.

✔ Learn that being too goal-orientated and impatient will only slow the process of your recovery.

✔ Develop a sense of kindness, patience and tolerance directed at yourself: this will enhance and speed up your recovery.

Recognise Your Own Progress

Our ability to acknowledge positive changes and signs of personal change can greatly enhance our sense of confidence and wellbeing.

Some of us do well at recognising and feeling good about progress and some of us are not so good at it. Most people are not good at it: that's a fact. So don't feel that you are the only one struggling with this, as it is a very common experience for us all.

Having said this, if we can begin to notice little changes that are happening in our mood, the way we think and the way we behave, this will give us a platform from which to grow further.

We cannot really grow and heal if we are unable to at least recognise in some way that we have made progress.

The interesting thing about progress is that it doesn't always feel good.

Let's say we have been suppressing some feelings and now, as we practise mindfulness. All of a sudden we begin to feel painful emotion. Now, this might not feel good or comfortable, but it is progress nonetheless, because we are allowing ourselves to feel that which we ran away from, which might in some way have contributed to our depression, and by feeling it more fully we are allowing ourselves to heal, grow through our condition, to a point where we can live well with it.

Attend Mindfulness Practice Groups

Connecting with others through group participation can deepen our mindfulness practice and by deepening our practice we can be in a better position to manage and heal our condition.

When we practise in a group we can begin to feel part of something greater than just our own efforts. This is because all the people in the group have the same intention and goal, namely to be mindful and open to the present moment.

It's the same when we walk into a room and the people in the room are angry and upset: we feel that very quickly. The same applies when we go to a place where all people are more calm and centred, going through a similar process of self-discovery.

Being in a group means you can

- ✔ Ask questions
- ✔ Share your experiences
- ✔ Hear other people's experiences (which might help reduce your sense of isolation)
- ✔ Socialise in a supportive and safe way

 If groups are not your thing, then perhaps find an online mindfulness group that has a blog type setting where you can leave comments and ask questions. Try typing **online mindfulness groups** into your favorite search engine and see what you can find. The choice is yours.

Talk about and Share Mindfulness with Others Skilfully

Talking about mindfulness to people who are interested and receptive can be a wonderful way of keeping the subject alive.

Not only that but it might give you an opportunity to begin to shift your attention from being too preoccupied with your own condition to sharing what you found useful with others. In this way, you may even begin to help those who are in some way stuck in their life.

It boils down to reminding that we have a choice of what we focus on. We can continue to keep ourselves stuck in unhelpful thoughts and share those with others or, we can explore and play with our capacity to choose what we think and do more skilfully.

Mindfulness is a very popular subject nowadays so it's a great conversation starter as well. Of course you don't aim to change the world, but the simplicity of sharing something of benefit has a certain potential for enjoyment and the feel-good factor.

Be Flexible

The reason why bamboo does not break is because it can bend with the wind and be flexible. It adapts to inner and outer change.

When we have depression, things might feel very set and stuck in our negative mental patterns and habits. Once we begin to practise mindfulness we can feel more relaxed and grounded. It is this sense of feeling more grounded in ourselves that gives us the ability to be more flexible and adaptable.

So if I were to tell you 'Come on now, be more flexible', you might tell me that you can't! And that is totally understandable. But I am not telling you to be anything. What I would like to invite you to do is to explore mindfulness as a practice, so that with time your capacity to be open, flexible and adaptable to change can grow.

Life is very uncertain. Things change, and this change can cause anxiety, but when you can find a place of peace and stability in yourself – and this place can be a simple awareness of a part of your body, such as your feet – you can be more resilient in the face of change. Just like bamboo, which has strong, deep roots, you will be affected by the winds of change, but you can stay strong in one place by simply bending.

Don't force yourself to be flexible, but give the practice a try and let this happen on its own, in its own time.

Index

About the Author

Robert Gebka is a former Zen Buddhist monk and the executive founding director of the Dorset Mindfulness Centre. He was born in Poland and spent most of his adult life living in South Africa before arriving in the UK in 2005. He now works in the mental health field for the NHS (UK's government National Health Service), where he facilitates mindfulness based interventions to people suffering from severe and enduring mental illness, including depression. Robert completed a five-year residency internship training in Buddhist studies, mindfulness psychology and Chinese culture at the Nan Hua Buddhist Monastery in South Africa. He studied meditation philosophy and mindfulness psychology with various teachers both from the Chinese Zen as well as the Tibetan Buddhist traditions. In 1999, he had the wonderful opportunity to meet His Holiness the 14th Dalai Lama, the blessing of which continues to inspire him today. He then went on to complete a two-year self-directed research project in Mindfulness Based Interventions within a UK NHS psychiatric hospital, facilitating groups to both patients and healthcare staff. Robert has shared life experiences of living with anxiety and depression and teaches mindfulness in a heart-centred and practical way that also draws on his personal insights and experience. He enjoys nature walking and speaks four languages, including basic mandarin Chinese and Polish.

Author's Acknowledgments

Above all I would like to express my sincere gratitude to my mother and father for providing the many wonderful causes, conditions and opportunities for my valuable life experience. I would also like to thank my mentors, teachers and friends, Venerable Hui Fang, Khenpo Choephel Rinpoche and Jonathan Stock as well as my spiritual mother Maria Atkinson for their continued guidance and mentorship. I would like to especially thank Dr Tim Devine for his clinical guidance; Linda Kinsella, not only for her friendship but also for all her healing sessions which helped me stay in the creative flow; Dr Yoann Buisson, our neuroscientist, for ensuring that the information presented in this book is scientifically sound and factually correct; and Helena Edwards above all for her warmth and support. A massive thanks also to Kristian Lees-Bell for his coaching sessions, my Dharma sister Kathy Monaco for reading through the book and giving me her extremely valuable feedback as well as Kim Thomas for all her information on nutrition.

Last but by no means least my gratitude to the Wiley team who guided me throughout the entire writing process ensuring that the book is presented in a readable and logical fashion.

Publisher's Acknowledgments

Executive Commissioning Editor: Annie Knight

Editorial Project Manager: Christina Guthrie

Development Editors: Simon Bell and Christina Guthrie

Copy Editors: Simon Bell and Christina Guthrie

Production Editor: Siddique Shaik

Cover Image: ©iStock.com/Borut Trdina

CN 4116